GARDENING BY DESIGN

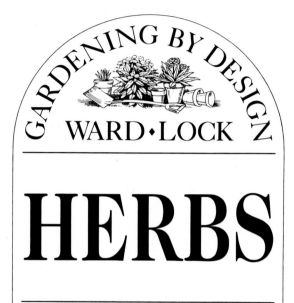

WARD · LOCK

HERBS

JANE COURTIER

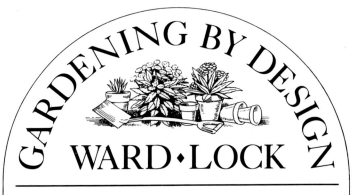

GARDENING BY DESIGN

WARD · LOCK

HERBS

JANE COURTIER

WARD LOCK

This edition first published in Great Britain in 1990
by Ward Lock Limited, Villiers House, 41-47 Strand,
London WC2N 5JE, a Cassell company

Reprinted 1990, 1991

House editor Denis Ingram
Designed by Niki fforde

Text set in Bembo Roman
by HBM Typesetting Limited, Chorley, Lancashire
Printed and bound in Spain by Graficas Reunidas

British Library Cataloguing in Publication Data
Courtier, Jane
  Herbs—(Gardening by design)
  1. Herb gardening
  I. Title II. Series
  635'.7   SB351.H5
ISBN 0-7063-6887-8

ACKNOWLEDGEMENTS

All the colour photographs were taken by Bob Challinor
with the exception of the one on p. 41, which was taken by
John Glover.
The publishers are very grateful to the following persons
and institutions for kindly granting permission for photographs of their gardens/properties to be taken: Arthur Billitt
Esq. (pp. 2, 6 & 10); Mrs R. Clay (pp. 15, 19, 21, 24 & 27);
the Marchioness of Salisbury, Hatfield House (pp. 31, 32,
35 & 38); the Royal Horticultural Society (p. 41); the
National Trust, Hardwick Hall (pp. 43, 71 & 75); Mr & Mrs
D. Simmons (pp. 47, 49, 51 & 53); Mr & Mrs R. Raworth
(pp. 59, 61 & 63); and Mr & Mrs W. E. Ninnis (p. 69).
All the line drawings were drawn by Nils Solberg.

CONTENTS

Gravel paths give all-weather access to the plants. Wooden surrounds to the beds ensure they remain well-defined: they also help to keep invasive herbs in their place.

1

INTRODUCTION

EARLY HISTORY

The history of herbs is as old as the history of man, for from the earliest times plants have been used by mankind for a whole range of purposes. The modern idea of herbs is a little different from the ancient one, where virtually any plant that had some useful property was called a herb. These days, defining herbs presents us with a bit of a problem.

Most people immediately think of edible plants which are used as flavourings for various foods. But then there are medicinal herbs, some of which, far from being edible, are extremely poisonous; there are fragrant herbs used to scent linen or rooms; herbs used as insect repellents; herbs for cosmetics; even herbs which these days have virtually no practical use at all but are still quite definitely identifiable as herbs. Many herbs have aromatic foliage—but not all. The botanical definition—a plant with no woody stem above ground —doesn't help us at all, for it includes many plants that are not herbs while excluding a good few that quite obviously are.

And yet most people are quite clear about what is meant by herbs (though there are still a few plants on the fringes which could cause a few arguments). The ancient definition still holds fairly true, for in the widest sense herbs are plants which have some use to man other than simple decoration.

The most important early application of herbs was in the treatment of disease. A Chinese herbal is said to have been in existence in 5000 BC; Egyptian papyri mention herbs in 2800 BC. The Greek physician Hippocrates set out many herbal remedies around 400 BC,

and it was another Greek, Dioscorides, who wrote *De Materia Medica* in Rome in the 1st Century AD — a manuscript that became a standard work of reference for hundreds of years.

It was the Roman invasion that brought to Britain many of our most popular herbs. As the invaders established new cities, they brought with them some of their most useful plants and tried to grow them in the villa gardens. Many survived the colder conditions and have been grown here ever since. For the Romans, herbs were not just medicinal; they were used lavishly as flavourings and in complex recipes.

After the fall of Rome, herbs continued to be grown in the 'physic gardens' of monasteries, their uses being set down in handwritten manuscripts. The invention of the printing press in the 15th century at last allowed herbals to reach a wider public, and one of the most famous and enduring was that of Nicholas Culpeper, published in 1652. Astrology still played a large part in these herbal 'cures', which had an aura of magic and mysticism—as well they might. They were frequently all that lay between life and death; sometimes they worked — sometimes they didn't.

The problem was that when they did work, nobody knew why or how the plants had their effect. In addition, it was impossible to tell how concentrated was the active ingredient in any one specimen; so much depended on when and at what state of growth the plant was harvested, how it had been grown, what the weather was like and many other variables.

The Doctrine of Signatures held that plants disclosed their own applications to those who knew how to read them. The spotted leaves of *Pulmonaria* looked something like diseased lungs—so they were used for breathing and chest ailments. Heart-shaped pansy leaves were thought to cure heart disease, and so on. It must have seemed as good a hypothesis as any other in those days.

As scientific methods developed and improved, it became possible to identify the active principals in plants, then to extract and purify them. Eventually it also became possible to synthesize them, and many modern drugs are now produced synthetically. It is surprising, though, how many potent drugs are still derived from plants such as foxgloves, monkshood, belladonna, henbane and lobelia.

The culinary use of herbs must have begun even earlier — when man discovered that the taste of one plant could be improved by the addition of a different plant. The uses of plants as flavourings and not merely as sustenance was one of the first aspects of civilization! The use of herbs in food preparation probably reached a peak in Roman times, when virtually every dish was heavily flavoured and spiced. A cookery book written by Apicius in the 1st Century AD has many extravagant recipes each containing large numbers of different herbs; lovage, celery seed, parsley, dill, savory, mint, coriander and cumin are among those still in common use today.

Over the years, the British developed a taste for plain, filling, simply cooked food and the use of herbs began to be regarded with some suspicion. Not so long ago, parsley, sage, mint and thyme were virtually the only herbs used in British kitchens. Even these were not used adventurously; parsley, sage and thyme were included in stuffings for roast meats, mint sauce accompanied lamb, and that was about it—apart from the occasional use of parsley as a garnish (usually uneaten, of course).

USING HERBS TODAY

Within the last 20 years or so, there has been a great change in our eating habits. As we have become more adventurous, sampling food from many other nationalities and cultures, so our appreciation and use of herbs and spices have increased. A wide range of dried herbs is available in every supermarket, and production of herb seeds and plants for sale has become a thriving industry.

Even more recently, we have been advised to steer clear of foods containing animal fats, and to avoid salt. Synthetic additives cause allergic reactions in some people; many others have an innate distrust of processed food heavily laced with chemicals. The movement towards natural, unprocessed foods, simply cooked, has brought with it an increased use of herbs to provide flavour and interest in the place of rich sauces, salt, and artificial flavourings.

The herbs themselves may well provide us with healthy benefits if eaten in sufficient quantity, as they contain vitamins and essential minerals, and frequently aid digestion.

Most culinary herbs contain essential or volatile oils which give them their aroma and flavour. The senses of smell and taste are closely linked and many herbs are pleasing to both. These oils are contained in special cells in the plant, and when they are ruptured, the scent disperses. This is why many herbs have no fragrance, or very little, until the leaves are rubbed or crushed.

Because the oils are volatile, herbs should preferably be used quickly, before the oils disperse. If the herbs are to be stored for later use, they need special treatment to preserve their flavour.

Herbs are often thought of as a safe alternative to modern drugs, and as 'natural' additives to food. In many cases this is true, but it should not be forgotten that herbs can also be potent drugs which must be used with discretion and care, while many plants that appear in old herbals (and even in present-day herb catalogues) are poisonous and should never be eaten.

The rule for using herbs in cookery is to stick to those you know are safe. If you are not sure that a certain plant is a culinary herb *make* sure before you try it. Use any new herb in fairly small quantities to start with while you decide whether or not you like it.

Using herbs for medicinal purposes can be risky. Not only is there the possibility of damaging your body by using the wrong plant, the wrong part of it, or the wrong dose, there is also the chance that a success-ful herbal self-treatment could mask the symptoms of a more serious disease. If you are under any form of medical treatment, consult your doctor before trying a herbal remedy, especially if you are taking prescribed drugs — they could react with the herbs.

Finally, make sure you understand *how* a plant is to be used as a treatment. Many are used externally and would be harmful if taken internally. However, there are many simple, safe and gentle remedies which can be used without any worries and are often quite effec-tive. These are certainly to be preferred to more power-ful drugs which can cause unpleasant side effects.

Herbs are the most satisfying plants to grow. It's not just their many uses, their attractive foliage and flow-ers, or even the tantalizing scents that are given off at the slightest touch that make them so rewarding. As much as any of this, it's the fascination of their long history, the knowledge that you are continuing a tradi-tion of growing plants that have been cultivated for centuries, that turns herb growing from an interest into a life-long addiction!

A pleasing pattern need not be complex, as this small formal garden at Clack's Farm shows.

2
DESIGN

From the intricate precision of an Elizabethan knot garden to a free-flowering wilderness of scented plants —a herb garden can be anything you like to make it. Before planting any herbs, it does pay to sit down with a pencil and paper and make some rough plans to avoid annoying mistakes later on.

OVERALL PLANNING

The first question is always — where? Most gardens have only limited space and the herb border must fit in with everything else. As a general rule, the nearer the house it can be the better. Here the scents can be more frequently appreciated, and there's not too far to go to pick the few sprigs that will make all the difference to a meal.

A sheltered position is always best. Most herbs are natives of warm climates and will grow more readily in a protected position; also, fragrances linger on warm, still air far longer than they do in a breezy, open spot. At the same time, plenty of air and sunshine are necessary for the majority of species, so shelter should not mean heavy shade. Which is the best spot for sitting out in summer? For that's probably the ideal position for your herb garden.

Once you've decided on the position, see how much space you can allow yourself. A large, formal herb garden can give a great deal of pleasure, but bear in mind it will need careful planning, be quite expensive to plant up, and it will take a lot of maintenance to keep it looking its best. However, few things are more irritating than being constrained by a tiny border

which it is impossible to extend sensibly, and collecting herbs generally becomes quite addictive!

Because shelter is so important, it's an excellent idea to enclose a herb garden with walls or hedges. You may be lucky enough to have an existing walled garden to convert to herbs — otherwise building walls from scratch is prohibitively expensive. Hedging can be arranged, though: it should be evergreen, preferably dark leaved to act as a foil for light coloured herbs, and not too greedy—privet, for example, will drain the soil of plant foods for a considerable distance, so that anything planted near it has a struggle to survive. Bear in mind that a formal garden means neat, well-trimmed hedges, with all the extra work that entails.

Fencing should not be despised, for although it does not look very attractive to start with, it can be much improved by climbing plants. It is relatively cheap and easy to erect, and could make all the difference to a garden in an exposed situation. Walls, fences and hedges all cast shade as well as shelter—another point to remember before putting them up.

Those gardens fortunate enough to be reasonably warm and sheltered do not need to be enclosed, and herbs can be planted out in the open.

Once you have decided on the position and size, you can get down to the detailed planning. Let's start with a large, formal herb garden.

FORMAL HERB GARDEN

The design of the formal garden is very important. The overall shape should be regular, divided into a number of equal sections to form a repetitive pattern. There should be a focal point; usually in the centre, though not necessarily.

The epitome of a formal herb garden is the knot garden, which is purely decorative. Bushy herbs in contrasting colours are planted to form low hedges which run through and over each other in complex patterns like ropes forming a knot. Knot gardens need to be viewed from above for the best effect: if you have a suitable garden—and an orderly mind!—they can be most effective and impressive, and are not as difficult to lay out as they look.

Knot Garden

The design shown in Fig. 1 is fairly simple. When planning a knot garden it really is essential to draw it to scale on paper first.

Plant the marked lines with suitable herbs such as santolina, wall germander, hyssop and lavender. Buy small but bushy plants and set them about 8–15 cm (3–6 in) apart, depending on size. At the planning stage, decide which 'rope' runs over or under at each intersection: generally each one goes under and over alternately to give an entwined effect. If you just impose the circle on top of the loops, on top of the diamond, this is not a true 'knot'.

Clip the newly planted 'ropes' back quite hard to encourage even, bushy growth, and trim the plants very regularly in the growing season. The spaces between the 'ropes' can be filled with pea gravel, shingle, flint chippings, forest bark or similar materials, using either one for the whole garden or, more effectively, several contrasting colours and textures to emphasize the patterns.

The knot garden is a masterpiece of precision, but it is not meant for cropping. A formal herb garden can, however, be both beautiful and useful.

The shape must be regular for the best effect, but can be anything within those lines: square, rectangular, diamond, circular, semi-circular, oval or triangular. The focal point is marked by something like a sundial or a white-painted, old fashioned beehive (with or

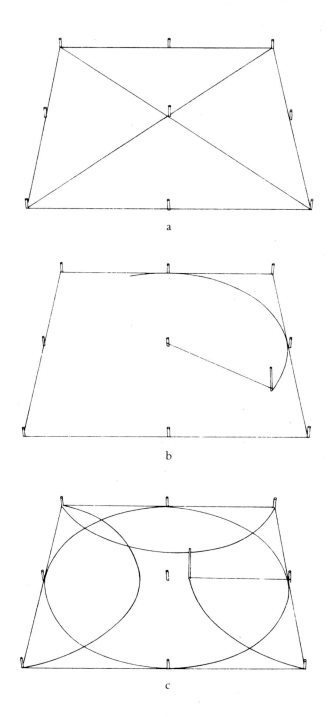

a

b

c

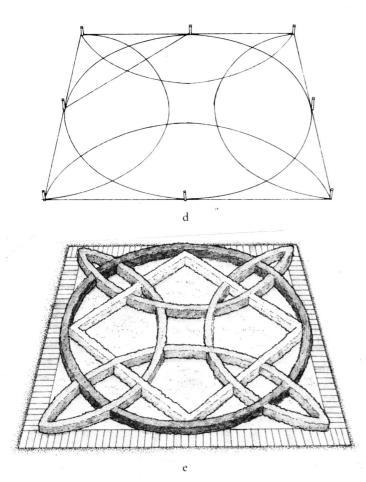

without occupants!), a small pool or fountain, a small evergreen tree or clipped shrub, an ornament or even just a large, striking herb like angelica.

Where the focal point falls is quite important, and depends on the shape of the garden, the direction from which it is approached, and many other factors. The dead centre of the herb garden is usually a safe bet, but if you can, try out some easily moved object in several different places, viewing it from all angles to see where it looks most comfortable. The natural focal point — the point to which the eye is most easily led — is not always where you might expect it to be. The rest of the herb garden design should radiate from that focal point.

Use paths to form the basis of the design. (They have a practical value, too, for you should be able to reach every herb from paved ground.) Two intersecting paths dividing a square garden into four equal parts is a pleasing, simple and well-tried pattern (Fig. 2). Where

Fig. 1 Knot garden (*a*) Mark the mid point of each side of the square. Stretch strings diagonally across to find the centre and mark it with a peg.

(*b*) Draw the circle with a stick and string tied to the centre peg.

(*c*) Move the mid point pegs slightly outside the square and use the stick and string, tied to these, to mark the semi-circles.

(*d*) Move the mid point pegs back to the edges and mark the diamond by running a stick along string stretched tautly between them.

(*e*) Use herbs in contrasting colours to plant up the 'ribbons'.

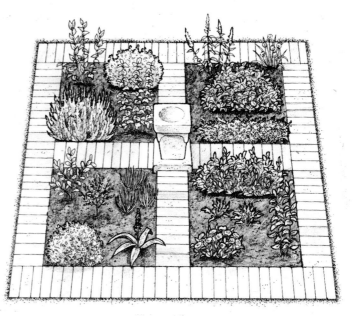

Fig. 2 A square herb garden with intersecting paths is a popular pattern. Add interest with a central focal point.

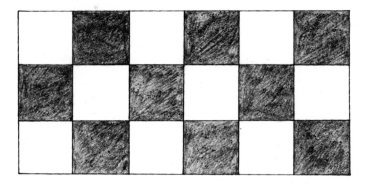

Fig. 3 Another simple design—a chequerboard of alternate paving slabs and herb plants.

they intersect, you can position a seat, sundial, small pool or what you will. Plant fairly low-growing herbs near the centre of the garden with the taller ones towards the back.

There are many more complicated designs you could work out for any particular shape, but remember not to make it too fiddly. Bold shapes and fairly simple patterns are usually the most effective.

For many people the herb 'garden' is, in fact, just a bed. This too can be of a formal design: one that is both practical and pleasing is a chequerboard of plants and paving slabs (Fig. 3). Don't try to cram too many herbs into each planting space—one reasonable-sized bush or perhaps two smaller subjects is usually plenty.

INFORMAL HERB GARDEN

Most herb beds are informal, whether by accident or design. In fact, these are even more difficult to make effective than formal plans. Many herbs have an annoying habit of not knowing their proper limits. The books might say 90 cm (3 ft) high by 50 cm (1½ ft) spread—but try telling that to the plant! In your soil it

may refuse to grow more than half that height while deciding to sprawl to double the spread. Or another compact, low growing variety might romp away to twice its normal dimensions, obscuring the more reticent, supposedly larger-growing plant behind it. In a small area where every inch counts, these mistakes show up badly, and there will be a continual juggling and shifting of positions until you find just how things grow in your particular site.

But an informal garden can be a beautiful, blowsy muddle where finding a choice plant almost hidden by another only adds to the charm, and the sheer exuberance of plants jostling for space more than makes up for their untidiness. There is a fine line between magnificence and messiness, though, and you will need to take care that your herbs don't escape your control. Fortunately many of them have no objection to being brought back into line by some drastic work with the secateurs before things go too far.

It's an unfortunate fact that truly beautiful informality can only be achieved by sheer good luck—unless you happen to be one of those people who have an instinct for plant associations and manage to hit the jackpot every time without knowing how they do it. For most of us, the informal garden needs a little basic planning to make it work. The following points about plants are just as relevant to plantings within the formal garden.

BASIC REQUIREMENTS FOR THE HERB GARDEN

The first essential is to know your soil and have at least a rough idea of the size each plant is likely to reach (though as I've said, this is not always easy). It might seem obvious but it's still worth saying—put the taller plants at the back and the lowest ones at the front. If your bed is viewed from all sides (an island bed) then the tallest herbs must go in the centre.

Many herb gardens look very bleak in winter. To

Herb beds need not be straight borders—an island bed is often more practical and effective.

give some visual winter interest (and provide fresh herbs for the kitchen in all months) make sure you have several evergreens, and use them to form the backbone of your planting scheme.

Then jot down the main season of interest of the herbs you particularly want to grow. Some appear very early in the spring (others so late that every year you're sure they've died). Some have brightly marked young foliage that fades as it matures: some reach their best in late summer when they are fully grown. There are flowers at various times from early summer through to autumn (though if you are growing herbs for culinary use you will probably cut these off, so don't rely on them for decoration). Then there are foliage colours—dark green, bronze, silver, steely blue, brilliant yellow—and textures; from finely divided to big and bold, soft and hazy to sharp and spiky.

Now you have to plan your planting so that all the different aspects complement, not clash. As to what's complementary and what's clashing—well, that's up to you! Basically you want to ensure the interest is spread right through the herb garden, not grouped together at any one season. You may wish to grade the colours, starting at one end with cool greys and blues, and working down through greens to warmer golds and reds, or you may prefer to have the different colours dotted about and evenly distributed.

TYPES OF PLANTS

Tall, bold, architectural plants are shown to their best advantage when they are accompanied by soft, fluffy foliage to form a complete contrast. In general, fine feathery foliage is best when used as a foil for the more robust-leaved plants.

So far I have only talked about the visual impact of herbs, but there are all sorts of other ways you could plan them to form a satisfying design. Group them according to their use—medicinal, culinary, household and so on—for an interesting and educational garden, or by scent, from citrus to spicy, sweet to sharp and pungent. A collection of herbs particularly attractive to bees will also attract butterflies and moths.

Although herbs are very often set apart and grown in their own plot, there's no reason at all why they shouldn't take their place amongst the border plants and shrubs. Many of them already do—rosemary, rue and lavender, for instance, are just as widely (if not more widely) grown as decorative plants as they are for any other purpose.

Make sure you know just where all the different herbs are and you can continue to gather them for use in the home, though you will have to be careful to pick shoots judiciously to leave a well-shaped bush.

Many herbs make particularly good edgings to beds, curled parsley, chives or dwarf lavender amongst them.

In small gardens, finding room for all the plants you want to grow is always a problem. Here, they must fit in as best they can, and every inch of space must be used.

HERBS IN PAVING AND IN WALLS

Because they can often grow in very dry, poor soils, herbs are naturals for planting in gaps in paving. Here there is the bonus of fragrance as they are brushed past or occasionally trodden on. Low, spreading plants are the most suitable. If you are laying a patio or path, leave slightly wider gaps every so often to accommodate plants: where different sizes of slabs are being used, leave one of the smaller ones out here and there. In existing paving you can often chisel out a small corner or squeeze plants in the gaps already there.

Walls offer similar planting sites (Fig. 4), particularly dry stone walls where it's easy to prod plants into cracks and cavities. The tops of walls can be planted, too, if sufficient soil is held there. As walls often provide exceptionally dry growing conditions, mix into the soil one of the water-retaining polymers now available in granular form.

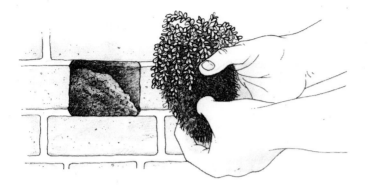

Fig. 4 Herb planting in a wall (*a*) When planting herbs in walls, carefully shape the rootball to fit the cavity.

(*b*) Put a little good loam in the hole and pack the roots in snugly.

(*c*) Several herbs are suitable for wall planting, but trailing thymes are particularly good.

Plants for walls and paving are best raised at home if possible. Cuttings should be rooted in very small containers and planted out while still young to ensure the root system fits oddly shaped crevices without too much damage.

RAISED BEDS

Raised beds are a convenient way of growing herbs, too. They can be constructed on a totally paved garden where they will give much better growing conditions than containers. They are useful where soil conditions are not the best for herbs — heavy, sticky clays for example — and provide the free-draining conditions many herbs love. Invasive herbs can be grown without fear of them spreading all over the garden, and weeding, picking and trimming become much simpler.

Raised beds are ideal for disabled gardeners (including the elderly) who have trouble bending or who garden from a wheelchair; blind gardeners will also appreciate the advantages of having scented and textured plants within easy reach and nearer nose level!

Make a raised bed as large as is practical, building it of materials sympathetic to the rest of the garden and the house. Choose the height to suit the purpose: 30 cm (1 ft) might be sufficient depth for most herbs, but if the raised beds are meant for wheelchair users obviously they must be much higher. Place rubble in the base if necessary to ensure good drainage before filling the bed with good quality, light loam (Fig. 5).

Raised beds dry out fairly quickly so they could need frequent watering in hot, sunny weather; try to position them within reach of a hose to make this easier.

HERB LAWNS

Many gardens—even small ones—give up quite a lot of their space to a lawn. Why not be different and try a herb lawn?

Fig. 5 Raised bed (*a*) Laying the first course of bricks.

(*b*) Filling the bed with compost.

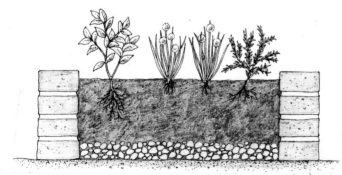

(*c*) Sectional view of planted bed.

I should say straight away that herbs won't give a close, even sward like turf. At certain times of the year they look distinctly patchy—and weeds can be a terrible problem. (You can't use the normal selective lawn weedkillers on herbs.) Added to which, they won't take the normal wear and tear, rough and tumble that grass does, and getting them planted and established takes not a little time (and money). But, against all that, a well-grown herb carpet can be such a beautiful and fragrant thing it's worth every bit of trouble, and more, that goes into it.

The best known 'lawn' herb must be chamomile, with its rich, fruity apple scent: it has been used for generations. The variety 'Treneague' does not flower and this makes it especially suitable; however, seed of this variety is not, of course, available, and establishing a lawn from plants is more expensive and labour intensive. The various creeping thymes are quite spectacular when in flower and will attract so many bees that walking on the plants is quite impossible! For a damp, shady corner, try one of the mints: pennyroyal or the tiny, creeping Corsican mint.

Keep herb lawns small. Prepare the soil for them very thoroughly, removing all weed roots: sow seed thickly or set plants about 10 cm (4 in) apart. Keep the new lawn well watered and weed it regularly, removing every weed you see. Once the plants have made good growth and knitted together they will help suppress weeds, but in the early stages it's up to you.

Once established, clip the lawns over with shears or use a hover mower to lightly top them: this helps to keep them close and compact. Occasional walking will do no harm, but a permanent pathway in a herb lawn will soon kill the plants in that area.

HERB HEDGES

Those herbs that do not mind being clipped make excellent formal hedges, while one or two make good, flowering, informal hedges and screens. As with all hedges, the soil should be thoroughly prepared before

An informal border filled with strong-growing plants; tall tansy and rosemary at the back, brightly variegated ginger mint in the centre and purple sage and savory in the foreground.

planting, being deeply dug, with a reservoir of plant food provided by the incorporation of well-rotted garden compost or animal manure, plus a long-lasting fertilizer such as bonemeal.

Buy young, well-shaped plants for a hedge. Most should be pruned back by about half after planting to ensure a bushy habit with plenty of new growth at the base of the hedge. As the plants grow, tip the sideshoots back lightly to keep them compact. Allow the plants to reach just above the required final height of the hedge, then cut the tops back to just below this height for a good finish. Trim according to the plant you are using: formal hedges require clipping two or three times in the growing season; informal hedges usually just once, after flowering.

Herbs suitable for close clipping can also be grown as single specimens, trimmed to a pleasing shape — something simple, like a pyramid or sphere, or more adventurous, like corkscrews or fantastic birds or animals.

While herbs like rosemary will make average size hedges, many can be grown as dwarf hedges to edge borders or form knot gardens. These miniature hedges need even more careful clipping to keep them bushy and compact: don't underestimate the amount of work involved in surrounding your herb garden or vegetable plot with a dwarf herb hedge!

HERBS IN CONTAINERS

If you have a really tiny garden, or even no garden at all, you may have to grow all your herbs in containers. More skill is needed to keep a container-grown plant happy and healthy, but many herbs adapt to this method of cultivation very well.

While they can be grown, if necessary, indoors, all herbs will do better outside even if it's only on a windowsill or balcony. Here they will receive better light and fresh air to keep them strong and sturdy.

Large containers for patios include half barrels, urns, large earthenware pots, troughs, sinks and tubs. Always use the largest container possible — it makes cultivation much easier. Any pot is liable to both waterlogging and drying out, so make sure there is a source of water close at hand.

Terracotta has a pleasant, rustic, warm look that goes well with herbs, but many of the beautifully decorated pots available today are liable to be damaged by frost. Unglazed terracotta absorbs water, a sharp frost freezes and expands the water and shatters the pot. In cold areas, choose frost-resistant pots, or keep them in a sheltered position. They can also be protected by lagging them with sacking, straw or loft insulation material.

Strawberry pots — urns with planting holes in the sides — offer great scope for trailers such as thyme. Separate containers for invasive herbs like mint will keep them under control, but mixed collections of other herbs can be planted in sinks, troughs and barrels. Don't cram too many in together, and choose the most valuable types, whether for scent, flavour, colour or general appearance. Steer clear of the very large, strong growers.

Since there is only a relatively small volume of soil in a container, plant foods will be used up fairly quickly. For this reason you might like to stick to annual or easily raised herbs that could be replaced, using fresh compost, every year — especially in small containers.

Just because you are restricted to growing herbs in pots doesn't mean you should forget design entirely. A mixed planting in a large tub must be chosen carefully, bearing in mind many of the same principles as for designing a large herb garden. Even a windowbox needs planning! A selection of herbs each in 10 cm (4 in) pots, can be arranged pleasingly and artistically in a window. The variegated or coloured-leaved varieties grow in pots just as well as their plain-leaved relatives —in fact many of them are slower growing and therefore more suitable.

The following tables indicate preferred locations, and soils for herbs, the types of foliage, what herbs are suitable for hedges, lawns, walls, paving and bees, and those growing under or over certain heights.

Positioning the herbs according to their likely eventual heights is important if they are all to be seen to their best advantage.

Table 1
Preferred locations and soils

HERBS FOR FULL SUN

Basil	Juniper
Bay	Lavender
Bergamot	Rosemary
Caraway	Sage
Coriander	Savory
Cotton lavender	Thyme
Hyssop	

HERBS FOR DAPPLED SHADE

Angelica	Lovage
Borage	Mint
Chervil	Parsley
Chives	Pennyroyal
Fennel	Sorrel
Lemon balm	Sweet cicely

*poisonous

HERBS FOR HEAVY SHADE

Comfrey	Valerian
Lily of the valley*	Violet
Lungwort	Woodruff
Tansy	

HERBS PREFERRING MOIST SOIL

Angelica	Elecampane
Bergamot	Lovage
Chervil	Mint
Chives	Sweet cicely
Comfrey	Valerian

HERBS WHICH REQUIRE WELL-DRAINED SOIL

Bay	Lavender
Caraway	Marjoram
Coriander	Myrtle
Cumin	Rosemary
Hyssop	Savory
Juniper	Thyme

Table 2
Types of foliage

HERBS WITH BLUE/SILVER FOLIAGE

Artemisia	Pinks
Cotton lavender	Rosemary
Curry plant	Rue
Eucalyptus	Sage
Lavender	

HERBS WITH VARIEGATED FOLIAGE

Geraniums, scented	Rue, variegated
Lemon balm, variegated	Sage, variegated
Marjoram, gold tipped	Thymes (several)
Mints (several)	

HERBS WITH DARK FOLIAGE

Basil, Dark Opal	Myrtle
Bay	Purple sage
Bronze fennel	

HERBS WITH FEATHERY OR LACY FOLIAGE

Anise	Dill
Caraway	Fennel
Chamomile	Parsley
Chervil	Southernwood
Coriander	Sweet cicely
Cumin	Wormwood
	Yarrow

*poisonous

HERBS WITH BOLD FOLIAGE

Angelica	Ladies' mantle
Burdock	Lovage
Comfrey	Lungwort
Costmary	Mullein
Dandelion	Nasturtium
Foxglove*	Rue
Hop	Sorrel
Horseradish	Thornapple*

Table 3
Herbs for hedges, lawns, walls, paving and bees

HERBS FOR HEDGES

Low:
Box	Southernwood
Cotton lavender	Wall germander
Hyssop	*Medium height:*
Lavender	Rosa rugosa (informal)
	Rosemary (formal)

HERBS FOR BEES

Bergamot	Marjoram
Catmint	Rosemary
Eucalyptus	Sage
Hyssop	Thyme
Lavender	

HERBS FOR LAWNS

Chamomile	Thyme
Corsican mint	Yarrow
Pennyroyal	

HERBS FOR WALLS

Hyssop	Sempervivum
Lavender Dwarf Munstead	Thyme
Rosemary (prostrate vars)	Wall germander
Savory	

HERBS FOR PAVING

Chamomile	Pink
Creeping mint	Thyme

Table 4
Herbs growing under 50 cm (1½ft) or over 2m (6ft)

HERBS GROWING UNDER 50cm (1½ft)

Basil	Marjoram
Chamomile	Parsley
Chives	Pennyroyal
Corsican mint	Pink
Cotton lavender	Lungwort
Lavender Dwarf Munstead	Thyme

HERBS GROWING 2m (6ft) OR MORE

Angelica	Fennel
Bay	Lemon verbena
Chicory	Lovage
Elecampane	Rose
Eucalyptus	Rosemary

Tansy *(Tanacetum vulgare)* has attractive finely cut foliage and yellow button flowers, but is very invasive.

3

GROWING AND PROPAGATING

SELECTION, PURCHASING AND SITE LOCATION

The common, culinary herbs are fairly easy to buy these days, though some of the more unusual varieties might give you a little more trouble. A good garden centre is the best place to start. Here you should find a reasonable selection of plants, usually in 5 cm (2in) pots, which will establish quite readily virtually all year round when planted out in the garden.

Selecting herbs is no different from choosing any other container-grown plant. You want a sturdy, bushy, healthy specimen of good shape; reject plants which are badly pot-bound, with diseased or pest-infested foliage, or which look drawn and 'soft' and have obviously been grown in protected conditions (unless you are prepared to harden them off carefully yourself before planting).

Check also (as far as you can) that the plants are correctly labelled, for misnaming of herbs is unfortunately common. If you are not familiar with any particular varieties you will have to buy them on trust, but check them out afterwards. It's always embarrassing to give another gardener a cutting of some especially choice herb only to have them tell you you've been nurturing some totally different plant for months!

Exchanging specimens with other herb enthusiasts is another good way of getting plants, especially some of the rarer ones. To start with, though, you will probably have to buy them from a specialist nursery.

There are increasing numbers of these all over the country, but if you cannot find one within travelling distance you will have to use the mail order service many of them offer. Plants are usually despatched in spring, but you will need to order as early as possible to be sure of receiving all the plants you want, particularly choice varieties. Postage is, unfortunately, expensive, but because plants are small, costs can be kept down to a reasonable level.

The site for the vast majority of herbs should be warm, sheltered and in full sun. It should also be convenient to the house, as culinary herbs need to be picked just before cooking if they are to retain all their flavour.

Exposed sites can be improved by protecting them with walls or hedges (see Chapter 2 for more details). One or two herbs grow better in light shade, so if your herb border can include a shady area, so much the better.

SOILS AND DRAINAGE

As a general rule, herbs are not fussy plants and they will grow in most soils and situations. A deep, moist, rich soil will promote plenty of lush foliage growth on most types, but the flavour will be inferior to those grown in poorer, dry soils. Many Mediterranean herbs in their native habitat grow in arid, dusty, stony soils so they are quite capable of coping with these conditions in the garden.

However, very poor, dry soils will not produce very attractive plants, and the plants will certainly not be able to cope with continual harvesting. So a balance must be drawn between good growth and good flavour.

Freely drained soils are essential for some herbs which quickly rot away in damp conditions. However, such soils should also be reasonably moisture-retentive to keep growth steady. This combination is not impossible, as it might first sound. It relies mainly on good soil structure, to allow drainage of excess water, and some organic matter (such as garden compost) to act as a sponge and hold some moisture in reserve.

Herbs require rather better drainage than many other garden plants. Free draining soils are composed of relatively large soil particles and are sandy or gritty. Heavy, clay soils, consisting of tiny particles which stick together and do not allow water to run freely between them, are the least suitable for herbs. The addition of plenty of organic matter will greatly improve their texture and drainage: working in sharp sand will also make them more suitable for herb growing. If you have a very light, sandy soil, add a small amount of organic matter to improve water retention and help stop plant foods being rapidly leached out of the soil.

Heavy applications of fertilizer are certainly unnecessary, but if you have poor soil, add a light dressing of bonemeal while preparing the bed, and incorporate this well. Bonemeal releases its nutrients gradually over an extended period, so will give the plants a steady supply of food without causing rapid lush growth.

In difficult growing conditions, due to bad weather or something similar, herbs might begin to suffer. In these cases a foliar feed sprayed over the plants will give them a quick boost and see them over the critical period. Regular fertilizing is not normally necessary.

PLANTING

Container-grown herbs can be planted at any time of the year except when the soil is frozen. However, it is not a good idea to plant them out in a very hot, dry period—wait until a cool, fairly showery spell if possible. This way they will establish much more quickly. Bare root plants — those lifted direct from the open ground — are planted in early spring.

Dig a planting hole large enough to accommodate the plant's roots freely. If you haven't been able to improve the soil in the whole bed, work some peat and sand or similar material into the bottom of the planting hole. It is vital to plant at the right depth—the crown must not be buried.

Firm the newly planted herbs well to ensure that the roots are in good contact with the soil, and if conditions are dry, water them in thoroughly.

For quick effect, plant closely using two or three plants of each species so that the herbs soon fill out and make the bed look established. Some perennials will then have to be removed after a few years as they grow and need more space, so bear this in mind when planting. It is cheaper to space the plants more widely to start with; you will have to wait longer for the bed to fill out, of course, and there will be more room for weeds between the plants, too.

WEEDING

As weeds compete with the herbs for light, space, moisture and nutrients, they should be removed as soon as possible, particularly while young herb plants are getting established. Hoeing is quick and efficient in dry weather, using a hoe with a very sharp blade to slice seedling weeds off at ground level (being very careful to avoid damaging the herbs, of course!). When the soil is damp, hand weeding is the answer—after all, as Kipling said 'half a proper gardener's time is spent upon his knees'! Hand weeding amongst herbs has, at least, the compensation of the various fragrances released as you brush against different plants, and gives you the opportunity to form a really close relationship with your herb border.

I suspect that most gardeners would rather not use weedkillers (or insecticides) among their herbs, but if

The soft colour of purple sage contrasts well with variegated ginger mint. In the background is a steel-blue rue and the pale pink flowers of chives.

you have no such objections, a paraquat/diquat mixture could be used (carefully) to kill off seedling weeds. This will kill the green parts of any plant that it touches. Perhaps the most useful weedkiller is glyphosate, as this will deal with the problem weeds, like bindweed, that are very difficult to control by any other method. This is carried throughout any plant to which it is applied, so it kills roots as well as topgrowth. Again, great care must be taken to keep this chemical off the herbs. Once you have eradicated difficult weeds like this, it should not be necessary to use chemical herbicides again unless the border is allowed to become very overgrown.

Weeds can also be kept at bay by using mulches. Make sure the soil is reasonably damp first, then apply a fairly thick covering of peat, pulverized bark or similar material. This will retain soil moisture as well as suppress weed growth. Well-rotted garden compost can also be used, though because this is not sterilized, as proprietary mulching materials are, there is more chance of it containing weed seeds and weeds will appear in it more quickly.

In reasonable soil, most herbs should not require much watering except while they are getting established: the moisture-loving types such as angelica may, of course, need more frequent watering in dry spells. The best time to water is in the evening, when the sun is off the plants.

PLANTING IN CONTAINERS

If you have only very limited garden space, or you want fresh herbs through the winter, you will want to grow some plants in pots. They are never quite as happy as they are when in the open ground, but with a little skill you can keep them growing well.

In a large outdoor tub (Fig. 6) which will not need moving about you could use garden loam or a loam-based compost; if you do need to move it, use a lighter, peat-based compost. Herbs will grow quite well in

either, though many gardeners swear by one or the other. I have always found peat-based composts give the best results, but if you prefer the loam-based, John Innes type, the herbs won't mind!

Make sure any container, large or small, has adequate drainage, with holes in the base and crocks over the holes: it's much easier to add water than to try to take it away. Drying out will, however, be a problem in dry weather and the smaller the container, the more difficult it will be to get the moisture level right. Be prepared for daily watering.

If you have no garden space at all, herbs can be grown in the house. If at all possible, keep them outside, on a balcony or even a windowledge. Otherwise, keep the pots in the lightest position available. They will all lean towards the light source, so every few days you should turn them round to keep them straight. Lack of light will lead to pale, drawn, sickly looking plants, and this will be a particular problem in winter, when light levels are low. Special horticultural electric light bulbs are available to supplement natural daylight: they are far more effective than ordinary or fluorescent lights because they transmit the correct part of the spectrum for plant growth. They are fairly expensive, but very worthwhile if you are trying to grow plants in a rather dim house (not everybody has nice, bright, sunny windowsills!).

If you want a variety of herbs indoors, 9 cm (3½ in) pots are probably the most practical size, though you should be prepared to replace plants as they outgrow these rather small containers. Use peat-based or loam-based compost, and give regular liquid feeds (any pot plant fertilizer will do). Keep the compost just moist at all times, and remember that overwatering kills more plants than underwatering.

Bringing potted herbs indoors is one way to keep fresh supplies available through the winter. Good pot subjects are parsley, basil, thyme, savory, marjoram and possibly (for a short time) rosemary and sage. If you have the facilities, raise seedlings in late summer for potting on and growing indoors in winter. This is more satisfactory than digging existing plants up and trying to pot them.

Fig. 6 Tub planting (*a*) Pour in gravel 1in (2.5 cm) deep.

(*b*) Pour in compost until tub is two-thirds full.

(*c*) Set the plant in the tub.

(*d*) Fill the remaining space with soil.

(*e*) Water the plant in well.

PESTS AND DISEASES

Fortunately herbs are not generally troubled by many pests and diseases. The point to remember is that strong, well grown plants are more resistant to pest and disease attack (though they are not necessarily less likely to be attacked in the first place). Because herbs are used in small quantities, a few insect pests can fairly quickly be washed or brushed off after picking.

Aphids (greenfly and blackfly) are likely to appear on any plant making soft lush growth, generally clustering near the growing tips. Because of their remarkably efficient method of reproduction, huge numbers can build up very rapidly. Watch out for them particularly on herbs which are growing in the house or greenhouse. Often the easiest method of control is to pinch out and crush the infested tips of plants. Another remedy is to spray with water to which you have added a small amount of detergent.

Lovage can be disfigured by celery leaf miner, a grub which tunnels within the leaves, leaving a thin ribbon of dead tissue. Pick off and crush affected leaflets. Parsley is often attacked by carrot fly. This small fly lays eggs in the soil near the roots of carrots, parsnips and parsley: the grubs which hatch out live in the roots, eating tunnels out of them. Because this reduces the efficiency of the plants' system for obtaining food and water from the soil, they soon begin to show symptoms of distress, though a minor attack will not produce very serious results. The older leaves begin to yellow and flag, and become tinged with red; plant growth slows or stops. Carrot fly attack is much worse in some years than others. It can be halted by using a soil insecticide (see precautions below). Raising two batches of parsley seedlings a year ensures you will have some replacement plants coming along. To some extent carrot fly can be carried over from one season to the next in the soil, so choose a fresh site or grow in containers of sterilized potting compost after an outbreak.

The most troublesome disease that's likely to attack your herbs is mint rust. This can attack all varieties of mint and is characterized by rusty orange, powdery spots on the undersides of the leaves. It has a very severe effect on plants and there is no cure. One way round the trouble is to lift some of the creeping underground stems in autumn, wash off the soil and immerse them in hot water, 44°C (110°F), for about ten minutes. This should kill the disease, but take care not to damage the rhizomes by allowing the temperature to go any higher. Rinse in cold water before replanting in a fresh bed of clean soil.

A different type of rust sometimes affects chives, especially in mild areas. If plants are badly affected it is best to destroy them and raise new stock from seed.

When using any chemical on edible plants, whether it is a fungicide or insecticide, you must take certain precautions. First read the instructions on the bottle or pack fully, making sure the particular chemical is suitable for use on edible crops, and if so, how long you must wait between application and harvesting. Wherever possible, choose a chemical that has a short interval between spraying and picking—some require only a day, while others could be up to a fortnight. Also, read the small print, where you could well find a list of specific plants that could be damaged by the chemical concerned.

PROPAGATION

Once you have your herbs established, you will probably want to increase your stock by propagating from them and there are various ways in which you can do this.

Seed

You can save seed from your own plants or buy packets of seed of the most common herbs from most garden centres. Seed always seems to be a cheap way of obtaining plants but this is not necessarily true. A packet of seed costs roughly the same as one small, pot-grown plant. If you use a seed tray and compost, you must add this to the cost: remember, too, that it will take several weeks before seedlings reach the same size as a bought plant. A packet of seed will of course give you a large number of plants, but if you want only one or two of each type of herb that's not much of an advantage.

Raising plants from seed is always satisfying, though, and many herbs grow very easily by this method. Many of the variegated or coloured foliage varieties will not come true from seed and must be propagated by other methods, so your choice of these is limited.

Early plants can be obtained by sowing in a frost free greenhouse in early spring. Fill a tray with sowing compost, firm and level it with a presser, then sprinkle

Hatfield House, Hertfordshire. An excellent example of a knot garden, with its repeated patterns and dwarf hedges edging the beds.

A dwarf box hedge makes a striking design against the white gravel in the knot garden at Hatfield House.

seed carefully and evenly over the surface (Fig. 7).
Cover lightly with a further layer of compost or fine
silver sand. Water with a fine rose on the can and cover
the tray with a piece of glass and a sheet of newspaper.

When the seedlings begin to appear, remove the
newspaper; when the first one touches the glass,
remove the glass. Water just sufficiently to keep the
compost moist, always using a fine rose. As soon as the
seedlings are large enough to be handled, prick them
out into another tray with more space between them,
or into individual pots. Handle them at all times by
their seed leaves — never by their stems.

When they have made sturdy little plants, they can
be planted outdoors. For bushiness, pinch out the
growing tip when the seedling is 10 cm (4 in) high.

Some herbs can also be sown outside, direct where
they are to grow—in fact some must be sown like this
as they dislike being transplanted. Rake the soil level
and break it down into small, even crumbs (Fig. 8).
Draw out one or two shallow drills with a cane in the
patch where you want your herbs to grow, then
sprinkle seed along these drills. Cover with soil, pat-
ting it firm, and label the patch. Water with a fine rose.
The herb seedlings will be distinguishable from the
weeds because they are growing in neat rows. Once
they are large enough, thin them out in stages to the
correct number.

Division

In spring, when plants that died down the previous
autumn are starting to re-emerge, many of the clump
forming types (such as chives) can be divided. Dig up
the entire plant with a garden fork and pull it to pieces
carefully with your hands, making sure every piece has
some strong, healthy shoots and good fibrous roots
(Fig. 9). Replant the section straight away. Many
plants are improved by regular division, making
stronger growth than if they had been left alone.

Cuttings

Softwood, semi-ripe or hardwood cuttings can be
taken according to the variety of plant. Soft tip

Fig. 7 Seed sowing in tray (a) Firming the compost in the
corners of the tray.

(b) Sowing seeds evenly over the surface.

(c) Covering the seeds with a layer of silver sand

Fig. 8. Using a rake, carefully pull the soil back over the newly sown seeds.

Fig. 9 Division of border plant (*a*) Lift the whole plant with a garden fork.

(*b*) Separate into smaller pieces by gently pulling apart.

(*c*) Replant the new portions straight away.

cuttings are successful with most herbs; semi-ripe and hardwood are suitable for shrubby varieties. Another method is root cuttings — used for horseradish.

Softwood cuttings are taken in spring and early summer. Choose healthy young shoots, and trim them to between about 5 and 10 cm (2–4 in). Cut the stems cleanly just below a leaf joint using a very sharp knife or a razor blade and remove the lower leaves. If you like, you can dip the base of the stem into rooting powder and tap off the excess to leave a light dusting, though this isn't essential. Insert the cuttings in a mixture of peat and sand or a sowing and cuttings compost and water them in well. Softwood cuttings must be kept in a humid atmosphere. Spray them with water in a hand mister, and cover the tray or pot with a clear plastic propagator top or even an inflated plastic bag. Gentle warmth will encourage rapid rooting: softwood cuttings root quickly anyway, sometimes within a few days.

Semi-ripe cuttings are taken later in the summer, when the stems have started to ripen at the base but are

Another view of the knot garden at Hatfield House shows how herbs can be grown for their flowers as well as their foliage.

still flexible. Take sideshoots of the current season's growth: if they are 15 cm (6 in) long or less, tear them away from the main stem with a small heel of older wood (Fig. 10). Longer sideshoots should be trimmed below a leaf joint with a sharp knife, making them 8–15 cm (3–6 in) long. Remove all the lower leaves and dip the base in rooting powder before inserting in a pot of sandy cuttings compost. Water in with a fine rose.

Semi-ripe cuttings are tougher than softwood and don't need so much mollycoddling. The best place for them is a garden frame out of direct sun. Keep the compost moist, but there's no need to provide the very humid conditions required by softwood cuttings. Rooting is not very fast: usually the cuttings are left in the frame (or a very sheltered spot in the garden) until growth starts the following spring.

Hardwood cuttings are a less usual way of propagating herbs but this method can be used for some shrubby types such as bay, rosemary and myrtle. The cuttings are taken in autumn, when the leaves have fallen on deciduous plants, and when plants are completely dormant. Take a well-ripened shoot of the current season's growth up to 30 cm (12 in) long, depending on the plant. Remove lower leaves of evergreens. Insert the cuttings to about half their length in light, weed-free soil in the open garden — one end of the vegetable plot is a favourite place — and firm them in with your foot. They can be left there for about 12 months. They root slowly but are trouble free.

Horseradish is the only herb that is commonly increased from root cuttings. If the large, fleshy root is dug up it can be cut into a number of sections with a knife, and each one will form a new plant.

Layering

This is almost like taking cuttings but without separating the cutting from the parent plant. Take a branch and bend it down to the soil; peg or hold it in contact with the soil with a stone. The underside of the branch can be nicked lightly to encourage rooting. Once roots have formed, the new plant can be separated from the

Fig. 10 Semi-ripe cuttings (*a*) Tearing off shoot with heel.

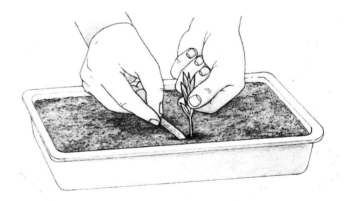

(*d*) Inserting cutting in tray.

parent, dug up and replanted.

'Mounding' is a similar method, where a spreading herb such as thyme is partially covered with soil in the centre. This holds down the branches all round, so that eventually large numbers of new plants can be separated.

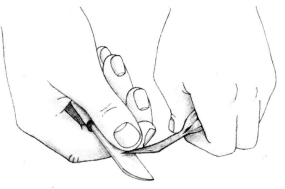

(b) Trimming shoot.

(c) Dipping shoot into rooting powder.

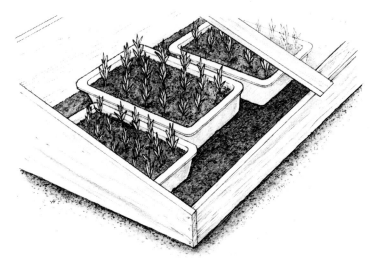

(e) Tray in cold frame.

(f) Rooted cutting.

Contrasting foliage colours between santolina *(centre)* and winter savory make this very simple bed effective at Hatfield House.

4

USING HERBS

You can start harvesting your herbs as soon as the plants are reasonably well established and have made enough growth not to mind the odd sprig being tweaked off. It is perfectly acceptable to pinch out the growing tips of quite small plants as this encourages them to become compact and bushy; however, it should only be the very tips of the shoots on young herbs—not half the plant!

It is the foliage that is most often used for culinary purposes. Just when you pick it and how it is used depends on the plant, but generally you should pick fairly young growth (though not the very newest shoots) which is fresh, unblemished and pest and disease free. Use it as soon as possible after harvesting—preferably within minutes as the flavour will then be at its best.

For most dishes where the herbs are to be eaten, they should be finely chopped as this ensures an even distribution of the flavour: in some dishes the whole, uncut herbs are infused into the dish and removed before serving. Even here it is a good idea to crush them lightly before adding them to the food, just to ensure the full release of their flavour.

Herbs are always best used fresh, but if you are to carry on using them in reasonable quantities through the winter, you will have to have a supply that has been preserved in some way. Because there is always some loss of flavour during the preservation process, you should gather the herbs when they are at their peak. This is generally just before flowering begins: choose a dry, sunny day and if possible pick them in the morning as soon as the dew has dried off the leaves. This is when the flavour should be at its strongest.

DRYING

Drying is the time-honoured—though not always the best—method of preserving herbs (Fig. 11). There are two schools of thought about the actual process. One is that flavour loss is kept to a minimum if the herbs are dried slowly in a reasonably cool atmosphere; the other that the drying should be completed as quickly as possible, using gentle heat. The problem with slow drying is that the herbs can get sticky and dusty (especially if they are hanging in the kitchen, which is the favourite place). A reliable method is to use a *very* cool

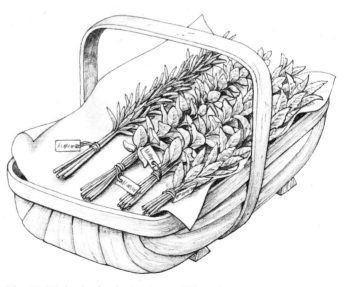

Fig. 11 Tie herbs for drying in small bunches.

oven—only just on—with the door open. Spread the herbs on cooling racks or greaseproof paper and turn them once or twice until they are quite dry and can be crumbled between the fingers.

HERBS SUITABLE FOR DRYING

Anise (seed)	Lovage
Bay	Marigold
Caraway (seed)	Marjoram
Coriander (seed)	Parsley
Cumin (seed)	Rosemary
Dill (seed)	Sage
Fennel (seed)	Savory
Hyssop	Tarragon
Juniper berries	Thyme

If you prefer to use the slow method, hang small bunches of herbs in a dry, airy place out of direct sun. Don't make the bunches large, or the centre of the bunch will remain damp and start to go mouldy. In very warm, dry weather, they will take only a few days to dry.

The flavour is preserved best if the dried herbs are left whole and crumbled just before using, but they take up more storage space like this. Once they are completely dry, they should be packed into small, tightly stoppered jars, crumbling them lightly if necessary. Keep the jars in a cool, dry cupboard, in the dark. It is better to use several small jars than one large one, because every time you take the jar out of the cupboard and remove the lid, a little more of the precious flavour and aroma escapes.

Seeds which are to be used in cooking also need to be stored dry, but these are allowed to ripen, very nearly, on the plant so that they are already dry when harvested. Because seeds have a habit of sowing themselves as soon as they are ripe, you must keep a careful eye on the plants as they approach maturity. Pick them when the first seed capsule has split open, cutting the whole stem. Be very careful when picking the stems, as a sudden movement can shower seeds everywhere! Hang the stems in bunches, upside down, with the heads securely enclosed in a paper bag: as the seed

capsules gradually split open, the seeds will be shed into the bag.

Seeds should also be stored in sealed jars. Don't crush them until you are ready to use them, as the flavour is preserved much more successfully in the entire seed.

FREEZING

In most households, freezing has taken over from drying as the most popular and convenient method of food preservation, and it's ideal for herbs—especially those with delicate foliage and flavour, which do not dry successfully anyway.

Herbs should be gathered when they are in their prime and frozen as quickly as possible. They can be left whole, in sprigs, and frozen in small plastic bags. When you are ready to use them, rub the bag between your palms and the frozen herbs will be 'chopped' for use. They are no good for use as a garnish once they have been frozen as they emerge looking very bedraggled.

One of the most convenient ways of freezing herbs is as ice cubes. Chop either single herbs or mixtures finely (Fig. 12), pack them into ice cube trays, cover

Fig. 12 Chop herbs finely with a sharp knife.

The Royal Horticultural Society gardens at Wisley include a well-designed and attractive herb garden. Note the use of a sundial as a central focal point.

with water, and freeze. Turn the frozen cubes out into polythene bags to save freezer space: a shot of soda water in each bag should stop the cubes sticking together. Just add one or two cubes to whatever dish you are cooking.

Herb butters can also be frozen; freezing them ready made is far more successful then trying to incorporate thawed herbs into butter.

HERBS BEST PRESERVED BY FREEZING

Basil	Dill	Parsley
Chervil	Fennel	Tarragon
Chives	Lemon balm	

HERB SALTS

Salt is a natural preservative and herb salts are very convenient to use. Again, you can use single herbs or make up a favourite mixture. Make sure any moisture has dried off the herbs you are using, then chop them well. Mix the chopped herbs with a good quality salt such as Maldon sea salt. The proportion of herb to salt varies according to the plant being used, but add as much herb as possible without making the salt too wet. Spread the salt and herb mix out on a baking tray and dry it in gentle heat. Break up any lumps that form before storing in airtight jars. Herb salt should replace ordinary salt on the table and in cooking; it has a very subtle flavour.

Herbs used for sweet dishes—such as sweet cicely, bay and angelica—can be mixed in a similar way with sugar. Caster sugar is best.

HERBS FOR HERB SALT

Basil	Marjoram	Thyme
Bay	Savory	

HERB SUGARS

Anise	Lemon balm	Scented geraniums
Bay	Mint	Sweet cicely

HERB VINEGARS

Use a mild-flavoured vinegar such as white wine, distilled or cider vinegar; the stronger flavoured dark malt will overpower the flavour of the herbs. Pack a jar or bottle with lightly crushed herbs and heat the vinegar (do not let it boil). Pour the hot vinegar over the herbs and seal the jar (don't use a metal cap). Shake occasionally and keep in a warm place for two to three weeks. Strain into a clean bottle and add a tall sprig of the herb you have used — this looks appealing and identifies the vinegar without the need for labelling. Use in mustards, mayonnaise and salad dressings; add sparingly to casseroles.

HERBS FOR VINEGAR

Basil	Lovage
Coriander	Mint
Dill	Rosemary
Fennel	Tarragon

HERB OILS

Good quality oil absorbs the flavour of certain herbs well. Pack a jar or bottle with lightly crushed herbs as for the vinegar and pour gently warmed oil over them. Cap loosely and leave in a warm place (a sunny windowsill is ideal), shaking or stirring frequently, and pressing the herbs. After two or three weeks strain the oil into a fresh jar of herbs and repeat the process. Herb oils can also be used in salad dressings, to rub on meat before grilling or barbecueing, in marinades, and to dress cooked vegetables lightly before serving.

HERBS FOR OILS

Basil	Savory
Fennel	Tarragon
Marjoram	Thyme
Rosemary	

Most striking in this group of plants at Hardwick Hall, Derbyshire, are the golden-leaved hop *(left)* and tall, white-flowered valerian *(right)*.

HERB MIXTURES

There are no hard and fast rules about which herb goes with which food, and you should experiment to see what appeals to you most. However, you might find it handy to have some ready-made-up mixtures of dried herbs available to speed up food preparation when you are in a hurry. These mixtures could also form a base to which you can add other herbs and spices as available.

FOR PORK

2 parts sage
1 part rosemary
1 part chives
1 part thyme
    or
2 parts juniper berries
1 part thyme
1 part lovage
1 part savory

FOR LAMB

2 parts rosemary
1 part marjoram
1 part lemon balm
    or
2 parts ginger mint
1 part fennel seed
1 part cumin seed

FOR GAME

2 parts juniper berries
1 part thyme
1 part marjoram
    or
2 parts caraway seed
2 parts sage
1 part lovage

FOR BEEF

1 part thyme
1 part marjoram
1 part sage

FOR FISH

1 part dill
1 part lemon thyme
Bay leaf
    or
2 parts lemon balm
1 part coriander
1 part anise
1 part sweet cicely

FOR POULTRY

2 parts tarragon
1 part savory
1 part parsley
1 part lemon thyme
    or
2 parts sage
2 parts parsley
1 part chives

USEFUL SPICES TO ADD TO HERB MIXTURES

Allspice
Cinnamon
Fresh ginger root
Mace
Mustard (black and white)
Nutmeg
Peppercorns (white, black and green)

Suitable for all meat and vegetable dishes.

CHEESE AND EGG DISHES

Cheese and egg dishes are usually delicately flavoured and herbs are often best used singly rather than in mixtures which could overpower the dish.

HERBS FOR CHEESE DISHES

Chives	Lemon thyme
Caraway	Lovage
Chervil	

HERBS FOR EGG DISHES

Chervil	Parsley
Chives	Tarragon

HERB RECIPES

Virtually any recipe can be adapted to include herbs. The following are a few ideas, some traditional, some new, that you could try. Don't be afraid to adjust the amount and variety of herbs to suit yourself. There are no hard and fast rules in herb cookery!

Two classic mixtures to start with:

Bouquet garni

Tie together a bay leaf, 2 stems of parsley, 2 sprigs of

Angelica archangelica: a statuesque herb whose leaves and stems are both used as flavouring.

thyme, 2 sprigs of marjoram. (If dried herbs are used, tie them in a muslin bag.) Add to casseroles, soups etc at the start of cooking and remove before serving. Rosemary, sage, savory or other herbs can be added or substituted as appropriate.

Fines herbes

Finely chop and mix equal quantities of parsley and chervil with half the amount of tarragon and chives. Add to dishes (especially egg dishes) just before serving. Always use fresh herbs.

Herb butter

Useful for serving in pats on vegetables or meat. Try spreading a split French loaf with herb butter, wrapping in foil and warming in the oven to make herb bread — a nice change from garlic bread.

Large bunch mixed dried or (preferably) fresh herbs —
   parsley, thyme, savory, marjoram, basil etc.
50g (2oz) softened butter
1 teaspoon lemon juice

Chop herbs very finely and work them and the lemon juice into the butter with a broad-bladed knife. Shape into a long block or roll, wrap in greaseproof paper and refrigerate or freeze until ready to use.

Herb stuffings

A stuffing or forcemeat is a traditional way of adding flavour to roast meat or fish.

SAGE AND ORANGE STUFFING
rind and flesh of half an orange
75g (3oz) wholemeal breadcrumbs
1 finely chopped onion
2 tablespoon chopped sage
salt and pepper
1 small egg
1 tablespoon vermouth (optional)

Grate the rind and chop the flesh of the orange and mix with the breadcrumbs, onion, sage and seasonings. Beat the egg with the vermouth if using, and add to the breadcrumb mixture. Use to stuff joints of pork or duck.

THYME AND SAVORY STUFFING
50g (2oz) wholemeal breadcrumbs
juice and grated peel of small lemon
1 tablespoon lemon thyme leaves
1 tablespoon savory leaves
1 tablespoon chopped chives
½ finely chopped onion
pinch of ground ginger

Mix all ingredients with sufficient water to bind. Shape into balls with damp hands, dot with margarine and bake in a moderate oven for 15–20 minutes.

Herb dumplings

250g (8oz) self raising flour
pinch of salt
125g (4oz) suet
2 tablespoons chopped fresh mixed herbs (or half the
   amount of dried mixed herbs)
water to mix

Sift flour and salt and add suet and herbs. Mix to a soft dough with water and with floured hands form into small dumplings. Add to soups or stews about 20 minutes before the end of cooking time.

Barbecues

The warm, spicy flavours of herbs are ideal for barbecues. Try laying a few branches of rosemary on the coals to give off aromatic smoke while the food is cooking.

The laundry museum at Eyhorne Manor, Kent, shows some of the herbs used to scent linen and clothes. The herb garden can be glimpsed through the open door.

MARINADE FOR MEAT
150ml (¼pt) red wine
1 tablespoon vegetable oil
1 shallot or small onion
1 tablespoon wine vinegar
bay leaf
3 sprigs thyme
2 sprigs sage
3 allspice berries
½ teaspoon chopped root ginger

Warm all ingredients together and allow to cool before using.

BASTING OIL
1 clove garlic
3 sprigs oregano
3 sprigs basil
2 sprigs rosemary
4 tablespoons vegetable oil (preferably herb flavoured oil)

Crush the garlic and lightly bruise the herbs. Put all ingredients into a saucepan and warm together for 10 minutes. Allow to cool. Use to brush on meat or fish before and during barbecueing.

Pasta

The bland taste of plainly cooked pasta is the ideal foil for herb flavoured sauces.

PESTO
large bunch fresh basil—about 75g (3oz)
pinch of salt
50g (2oz) pine kernels
2 garlic cloves
50g (2oz) grated Parmesan
4–5 tablespoons olive oil

Pound basil, salt, pine kernels and garlic cloves in a pestle and mortar. Add Parmesan, then gradually add the oil until it is well blended. A blender or food processor can be used to amalgamate all the ingredients instead. Store in a refrigerator: stir through freshly cooked pasta.

TOMATO SAUCE
1 rasher streaky bacon or 25g (1oz) vegetable margarine
1 garlic clove
1 small onion
500g (1lb) ripe tomatoes
½ teaspoon brown sugar
salt and pepper
1 tablespoon chopped fresh oregano
1 tablespoon chopped fresh basil

Chop bacon and cook over a low heat to extract the fat, or melt margarine. Add crushed garlic clove and finely chopped onion; cook until soft but not brown. Roughly chop the tomatoes (skinned if you prefer) and cook until thoroughly softened. For a smooth sauce, blend and sieve. Season, add the sugar and stir in the herbs.

Salads

Finely chopped herbs of all sorts can be sprinkled over salads or mixed with dressings. Make oil and vinegar dressings with herb vinegar, or try this attractive mayonnaise.

GREEN MAYONNAISE
6 stems of watercress
6 stems of parsley
12 large sorrel leaves
300ml (½pt) mayonnaise

Pour boiling water over the herbs and leave them for 5 minutes. Drain thoroughly, add to mayonnaise and blend in a liquidizer.

Herb jellies

Mint jelly is the best known, and infinitely superior to mint sauce. Sage or rosemary can also be used.

2.5kg (5½lb) cooking apples or crab apples
large bunch of fresh mint
1.3 l (2¼pt) water
1.3 l (2¼pt) vinegar
sugar
8 tablespoons finely chopped mint leaves

A close-up of the herbs shown in the previous photograph: *(upper step)* lavender and melilot (fresh and dried); *(lower step, rear)* dried woodruff, dried thyme; *(lower step, middle)* pomanders, rosemary, costmary; *(lower step, foreground)* feverfew, eau-de cologne mint, southernwood *Artemisia abrotanum*, and a home-made pot pourri.

49

Chop the apples and put in a large pan with the bunch of whole mint. Cover with the water and simmer until the apples are soft, then add the vinegar and boil for a further 10 minutes. Strain through a jelly bag. Measure the amount of juice and add 450 g (1 lb) sugar to every 500 ml (1 pt) juice. Boil until setting point is reached. Remove from the heat and allow to cool for about 10 minutes before stirring in the chopped mint. Pour into warm jars and seal.

Apple fool

This can also be made with gooseberries or rhubarb.

250 g (½ lb) apples
1 tablespoon chopped sweet cicely
honey
small carton double cream or plain yogurt
1 egg white

Peel and chop the apples and cook them with sweet cicely until pulped. Add honey to taste (be careful not to add too much). Fold in the whisked cream or yogurt and the stiffly beaten egg white. Chill. Decorate with candied angelica.

POT POURRI

The scent of summer flowers can be preserved all year round by making *pot pourri*. There are two methods, moist and dry. Moist *pot pourri* has a better, longer lasting fragrance, while dry *pot pourri* has a more attractive appearance.

The basis of most *pot pourri* is rose petals. Old-fashioned roses are best, but any highly scented variety will do. Collect the petals when the flowers are at their peak. Add whatever other scented flowers and leaves are available, together with some spices, and a fixative to preserve the scent—gum benzoin and orris root are the most readily available.

For dry *pot pourri*, spread the petals and leaves on newspaper or a drying frame in an airy room to dry slowly until they are crisp before mixing them. For moist *pot pourri*, leave them to dry for only one or two days, until they are limp.

Varying the proportions of the different flowers, foliage and spices will give very different fragrances.

Dry pot pourri

Store dried petals and leaves separately in airtight containers until you have enough, then tip them into a large mixing bowl. To each 2 litres (½ gallon) add 1 teaspoon each of finely ground cinnamon, allspice and cloves, and one bay leaf torn into pieces. Mix thoroughly, then add 8 g (¼ oz) gum benzoin and 30 g (1 oz) orris root powder. Store in a tightly closed jar, shaking daily, for about two months, then tip into containers. The two months' storage is necessary to allow the full fragrance to develop.

Moist pot pourri

Dry petals and leaves for one or two days until they are limp and leathery. Pack into an earthenware jar or similar container to make a layer about 10 cm (4 in) deep, then cover with rock or sea salt to about 5 mm (¼ in). Add further layers as materials are available, stirring the contents of the pot first. Weight the *pot pourri* down after adding each new batch if possible. At the end of the season, break up the mixture and add dried orange peel, cloves, cinnamon, mace, bay leaves, orris root powder and a small amount of brandy to moisten. Put it back in the jar, pressing well down, weight it and leave it to mature for several months.

Pot pourri should be kept in closed jars, with the lids taken off as required to scent the room: this way their aroma lasts much longer. In open bowls they will have a shorter life, but can be stirred occasionally and revitalized with essential oils if necessary.

The laundry museum at Eyhorne Manor displays a fascinating array of old implements. On the dresser are numerous irons used for different purposes: to crimp collars, hatters' irons and even an early oriental iron from the Ch'ing dynasty. To the right, on the pillar, are some interesting trivets.

Suitable ingredients for pot pourri

FLOWERS

Roses, carnations, lavender, pinks, jasmine, stocks, wallflowers, honeysuckle, lily of the valley, philadelphus, thyme, bergamot, mignonette, myrtle, violets, heliotrope, choisya, peonies.

LEAVES

Thyme, lemon verbena, scented geraniums, mint, rosemary, bay, sweetbriar, lavender, southernwood, sweet cicely, lemon balm, bergamot, myrtle, choisya, sage, costmary, eucalyptus, marjoram, chamomile.

SPICES

Allspice, cinnamon, mace, coriander, cloves, nutmeg, aniseed.

This is not a complete list — virtually any scented flower or leaf can be added to a pot pourri.

SACHETS

Make up small muslin sachets and fill with dried herbs such as lavender or dry *pot pourri* mix to store among linen or to hang in the wardrobe. Use a mixture of insect-repellent herbs to keep moths away — mint, rue, cotton lavender, rosemary, tansy, southernwood and wormwood.

Remember that the fragrance does not last for ever — you should make up new sachets every year.

HERB PILLOWS

Use a double thickness of cotton to make a pillow slip, to prevent dust from the herbs from escaping from the pillow. Dried hops are traditionally used to ensure sound sleep, otherwise fill the pillow slips with any pleasantly scented, dried mixture.

HERB BATHS

To scent a bath, make a muslin bag containing your chosen herbs plus a tablespoon of oatmeal. Hang this from the hot tap so that the water runs through it. Alternatively, pour boiling water over a handful of bruised herbs in a large jug, leave it to brew, then strain into the bathwater. Good bath herbs are rosemary, mint, lemon verbena, chamomile, peppermint.

SIMPLE SKIN CREAM

500g (1lb) pure clarified lard or petroleum jelly
Elderflowers, stripped from their stems

Melt the lard or petroleum jelly and pack in as many elderflowers, pressed well down, as can be covered. Keep on a very low heat (do not boil) for an hour. Strain into jars. Use as a soothing and protecting hand and face cream.

MEDICINAL HERBS

Many herbs have strong medicinal properties, but self-medication is not recommended. Apart from the dangers of overdosing or even poisoning, there is a risk of herbal treatments masking the symptoms of a more serious disease. Illnesses and recurrent problems should always be taken to your doctor.

Herbal teas (in moderate amounts) are pleasant and refreshing to drink and can help to alleviate the symptoms of simple illnesses like colds or stomach upsets. Pour boiling water on to dried or lightly crushed fresh herbs and leave to infuse for about 10 minutes. Strain. Add lemon juice and honey to taste.

Rosemary, peppermint, lemon verbena, elderflowers, sage, lavender, chamomile and rose hips make good teas.

Some of the laundry herbs at Eyhorne Manor. Clockwise from bottom left: lavender, melilot (dried), melilot (fresh), rosemary, costmary, mint, mixed dried herbs *(in trug)*, southernwood and (centre) feverfew.

HERBS

TO ALLEVIATE COLDS AND COUGHS:

Chamomile	Mallow
Fennel	Rosemary
Garlic	Sage
Horehound	Thyme
Hyssop	

TO AID THE DIGESTION:

Anise	Dill
Caraway	Fennel
Chamomile	Marjoram
Coriander	Peppermint

MILD DIURETICS:

Parsley	Savory
Sage	Tarragon

POISONOUS HERBS:

Belladonna	Henbane
Bryony	Lily of the valley
Foxglove	Monkshood
Hemlock	Thornapple

Melissa officinalis aureus: golden variegated balm. This easily grown plant adds a splash of bright colour to the herb garden. The leaves have a distinct lemon scent and flavour.

The bright blue, nodding flowers of borage *(Borago officinalis)* are extremely attractive to honey bees. Both the flowers and the rough, hairy leaves taste of cucumber.

5

A-Z SELECTION OF POPULAR HERBS

ANGELICA
Angelica archangelica (Umbelliferae)
Biennial or short-lived perennial
Angelica is a majestic herb, commonly growing from 2–2.5 m (6–8 ft) tall. When grown from seed, in the first year a small rosette of leaves is all that appears. In the second or perhaps third year, the thick, hollow flower stems shoot up, carrying great cartwheels of tiny, sweet-smelling, pale green flowers in early summer. Leaves in the second year are larger, with broad petioles, and are divided into leaflets.

Wild angelica is a plant of woodland and river banks, and the cultivated variety retains the preference for rich, moist soil and a lightly shaded position. The life of the plant is prolonged if the flowerheads are cut off before seed is set: self-sown seedlings appear in large numbers if the seed is allowed to fall naturally.
Uses: Stems, leaf stems, root, seed and leaves are all used, though the candied stems are the most familiar. All parts are pleasantly aromatic, particularly the seeds, which are used to flavour drinks including gin and vermouth. The leaves and roots can be added to stewed fruit to reduce its acidity.

ANISE
Pimpinella anisum (Umbelliferae)
Annual
A sweet, aromatic herb with a very distinctive flavour, anise is a native of Mediterranean regions. The plant grows from 45–60 cm (1½–2 ft) with rounded, lobed basal leaves having serrated edges, and feathery, finely cut upper leaves on the flower stems. Flowers are small and cream, held in typical umbels appearing in July and August. They are followed by pale brown, ribbed seeds which are widely used as a flavouring.

Anise likes a warm climate and seeds do not ripen well in northern regions. In cold areas, sow the seeds in fibre pots in a greenhouse in early spring, planting the complete pot outside in a sunny position after the risk of frost is over. Otherwise sow direct in a sunny spot after frosts have finished; mark the position as anise is slow to germinate.
Uses: Ripe seeds are used as flavouring for sweet dishes and in curry mixtures; they have medicinal value as an aid to digestion, and they help soothe coughs. Their most important commercial use is in *pastis* such as Pernod, and liqueurs. The foliage can be added to fish dishes or used in salads.

BALM
Melissa officinalis (Labiatae)
Perennial
Another Mediterranean native, but one that grows well in both northern and southern climates. Lemon balm, or bee balm, is a bushy herb reaching around 60 cm (2 ft). It has bright green, rounded leaves which are wrinkled and rough: a variegated variety, splashed with yellow, is known as golden balm. White, nettle-like flowers appear in midsummer and are very attractive to bees.

Plants can be raised from seed, cuttings, or by division. They will grow in most soils, though a reasonably moist position is preferred.
Uses: Leaves have a strong, pleasant citrus scent, and

can be used in any dishes where a lemon flavour is appropriate. They make a refreshing herbal tea which helps relieve headaches. Balm is best used fresh for culinary purposes, but dried leaves can be added to *pot pourri* or stored with linen both to scent it and to repel insects. Harvest the stems just before flowering; the aroma is very volatile and is soon lost.

BASIL
Ocimum basilicum (Labiatae)
Annual
Sometimes called king of herbs, basil grows to around 45 cm (1½ ft), forming a bushy plant with smooth, light green, tender leaves and spikes of small white flowers. 'Dark Opal' is a particularly attractive variety with deep purple foliage. Basil likes a warm climate, and in cool areas seed should be raised in a greenhouse in early spring, plants being set out after frosts are over.

Grow basil in a sunny spot on free draining soil: sow more seeds outside in summer to ensure a succession of young plants. Pinch out flowering shoots to promote leafy growth.
Uses: The foliage is very pungent, with a warm, sweet, spicy scent similar to cloves. It is traditionally used with tomatoes, but can be added to many savoury dishes.

As basil has a powerful flavour it should be used with discretion; the fresh foliage is far superior to dried. Basil aids the digestion and stimulates the appetite: sniffing the crushed foliage helps to clear the head. A few basil leaves added to a *pot pourri* give it a pleasant, spicy fragrance.

BAY
Laurus nobilis (Lauraceae)
Perennial
This rather tender evergreen tree has lanceolate, shiny, deep green leaves. It can grow to around 9 m (30 ft) in warm climates, but is very amenable to clipping and is often grown trained as a standard or pyramid. Fluffy white flowers in early summer are followed by black berries.

Plant bay in a sheltered position on light, well-drained soil. In cold areas, grow plants in tubs so that they can be taken indoors in cold spells. Propagate from soft or semi-ripe cuttings in summer. Watch out for scale insects on the undersides of the leaves—these eventually lead to disfiguring sooty mould growth.
Uses: The mature leaves are dried and used whole in soups, stews, sauces and rice pudding; they also form part of a *bouquet garni*. Tear the edges of the leaves before use. They have a powerful flavour and dry well. Remove them from the dish before serving. In Greek and Roman times, a 'laurel wreath' (of bay) was an award of honour. .

BERGAMOT
Monarda didyma (Labiatae)
Perennial
A decorative plant from North America, bergamot stands about 90 cm (3 ft) high with long, toothed, mid-green leaves. Flowers appear in midsummer in shaggy, scarlet whorls; there is also a pink-flowered variety. Bergamot prefers a rich, fairly moist soil with some organic matter such as garden compost added. It can be grown from seed, but is more usually propagated by division in spring.
Uses: The leaves have a strong, rich, citrus fragrance and can be used to make tea. This was a common drink of the Oswego Indians and has given bergamot its alternative name of Oswego tea. The foliage is an excellent addition to a *pot pourri*. Leaves can be dried throughout the summer; they are at their most fragrant if picked just before flowering.

Bergamot is a favourite plant of bees, who visit the lipped flowers whenever they are open. The bergamot oil of perfumery is derived not from this plant, but from the Italian bergamot orange which has a very similar fragrance.

BORAGE
Borago officinalis (Boraginaceae)
Annual
This fast growing plant quickly reaches around 90 cm (3 ft) high, with a very hairy stem and rough, wrinkled, bristly leaves. The flowers are star-like, pink in

Lavender *(left)* is an excellent plant with which to edge a path. The strongly fragrant flowerheads have been used for centuries to scent linen.

bud, becoming brilliant blue on opening, with prominent black anthers. The flowers characteristically hang their heads.

Borage is a hardy annual and very easy to grow on virtually any soil. It seeds itself with great enthusiasm, but the tough-looking seedlings, with their large seed leaves, are easy to spot and rogue out if they are not wanted.

Uses: The foliage has a refreshing cucumber flavour and is often used in summer drinks, especially fruit cups. It can also be used in salads, but pick only the young leaves, before they become too hairy. The bright blue flowers have a similar mild flavour and can be added to salads or used to decorate cold dishes; they can be floated on drinks or frozen into ice cubes. Borage has an age-old reputation as a promoter of cheerfulness and courage.

CARAWAY
Carum carvi (Umbelliferae)
Biennial
Caraway has pale green, feathery, divided leaves: in its second year it produces heads of pinkish white flowers which are followed by dark brown, ridged seeds. If the flower stems are removed the plants can be kept growing for another year but they self-seed readily if allowed too, ensuring a perennial supply.

Seeds can be sown in spring or autumn in any moderately rich soil in a sunny position. Self-sown seedlings should be thinned out as soon as they can be identified. Plants grow to around 60 cm (2 ft).

Uses: The seeds are the most strongly flavoured part of the plant, with a warm, spicy, characteristic taste and aroma. Familiar as the flavouring for 'seed cake', they are also widely used in bread and biscuits, and with cabbage in the German *sauerkraut*.

The foliage and stems can also be used, having a flavour similar to, but milder than, the seeds. They are especially suitable for fish and cheese dishes, and are good in salads, too. Caraway seeds aid digestion, so they are often eaten with rich foods. They are used commercially as a flavouring for *kummel* and other liqueurs.

CHAMOMILE
Anthemis nobilis (Compositae)
Perennial
This low-growing, creeping plant goes under several other Latin names, the commonest being *Chamaemelum nobile*. It has finely divided, apple-scented, ferny leaves and daisy-like white and yellow flowers which stand about 30 cm (1 ft) tall.

Chamomile is frequently grown as a lawn substitute, sometimes in the mistaken belief that it is labour saving. Small chamomile lawns can be effective and pleasantly aromatic, but need painstaking hand weeding while they are getting established. They will stand less wear than grass. The variety 'Treneague' is best for lawns — it is neater because it does not flower.

Chamomile likes a well-drained position in full sun. Ordinary varieties can be raised from seed but 'Treneague' must be propagated by division of the runners.

Uses: Chamomile has no real culinary use, but the fresh or dried flowerheads can be made into a tea which is taken for stomach upsets, headaches or colds. It can also be applied externally to soothe minor wounds, and forms a pleasant rinse for light-coloured hair. Commercially it is used in some cosmetic preparations.

CHERVIL
Anthriscus cerefolium (Umbelliferae)
Annual
Chervil is a dainty, fragile-looking plant, with pale green, lacy leaves and small umbels of delicate white flowers. It grows to between 60 and 90 cm (2–3 ft) on lightly shaded, moisture-retentive soil.

Chervil should be sown several times in a season, starting in late spring and continuing until midsummer for a succession of leafy plants. Sow where it is to grow, as the plants resent root disturbance. If seedheads are allowed to form the plant will sow itself readily, but to promote maximum foliage growth the flowering stems can be removed.

Uses: The soft foliage has a fresh, delicate flavour of aniseed. It disperses very quickly, so the herb should be

This small, formal garden benefits from the shelter of tall beech hedges. Fragrant lilies add height to the low-growing herbs.

used as soon as possible after harvesting and must be added to cooked dishes just before serving. It is particularly good with fish and eggs, and in salads.

Chervil also makes a pretty garnish for delicately flavoured dishes, in place of the more robust tasting parsley.

CHIVES
Allium schoenoprasum (Liliaceae)
Perennial
Chives are the smallest and prettiest member of the onion family, growing to about 22–30 cm (9–12 in) tall. The grass-like leaves are cylindrical, tapering and hollow, forming large clumps with small bulbs just below the surface of the soil. In summer, round, pink, papery flowers are produced. While these are very decorative, they should be removed to stimulate maximum foliage growth. The answer is to grow two clumps, allowing one to flower and keeping the other for culinary use.

Chives are easily grown from seed, and once established the clumps should be divided every two or three years in spring. If yellow, withered leaves appear, water the plants with a liquid feed. Chives like a fairly moisture-retentive soil.
Uses: Chives have a delicate onion flavour and can be used in any dish where this is appropriate. Their mild flavour is particularly suitable in salads, with eggs and cheese, and as a garnish for soup. Chop finely, and add to dishes shortly before the end of cooking.

CORIANDER
Coriandrum sativum (Umbelliferae)
Annual
The divided, mid-green leaves—broad at the base and finer towards the top of the plant—and small, pinkish white flowers are typical of the umbellifer family. The flowers are followed by clusters of round, brown, strong-smelling seeds.

Seeds of this 60 cm (2 ft) hardy annual can be sown in autumn or early spring in free-draining soil in a sunny position. Sow where the plants are to grow, as they do not like root disturbance.
Uses: The foliage and unripe seeds have a very strong, penetrating scent which some people find unpleasant: it is warm and spicy but difficult to describe accurately. When ripe, the seeds lose some of these unpleasant undertones, and these, together with the fresh leaves, are widely used in Indian cookery. They are suitable for any strongly spiced savoury dish, particularly curries.

Coriander is thought to have a beneficial effect on the digestion.

COSTMARY
Balsamita major (Compositae)
Perennial
This plant has long, pale green leaves with toothed edges, and small yellow flowers. It grows to about 90 cm (3 ft) but tends to sprawl unless supported. Its general weed-like appearance is reinforced by the fact that it is very invasive. The roots should be restricted to prevent costmary taking over the whole herb bed.

It can be raised from seed, but once established is easily increased by division in autumn or spring. Well-drained soil is preferred.
Uses: Costmary is also known as alecost and bible leaf: alecost because it was once used to flavour beer (like hops) and bible leaf because the pressed leaves were used as scented bible bookmarks. They have a sweet, spicy fragrance rather like balsam and can also be stored amongst linen and in *pot pourri*. It has insect repellent properties.

Costmary is not much used as a culinary herb but can be added in very small amounts to strongly flavoured dishes.

CURRY PLANT
Helichrysum angustifolium (Compositae)
Perennial
A small, evergreen shrub growing to about 60 cm (2 ft) with narrow, needle-like silvery leaves: a good decora-

Herbs can be mixed with border plants. The ornamental grey-leaved *Stachys lanata* blends well with cream and green variegated apple mint in the left foreground.

tive plant grown for its bright effect. Flowers are yellow, button-like and not particularly decorative. They are produced from midsummer. Plant in full sun in light, free-draining soil. The curry plant can be propagated from tip cuttings during the summer months.

Uses: The foliage of this plant gives off a warm curry scent not just when the foliage is touched, but when it is in hot sunshine. It is a pleasant fragrance which carries for some distance. The flavour is not as strong as the scent, but a few sprigs can be added to delicately flavoured foods to give them a mild, spicy aroma. Dried leaves can also be added in very small quantities to a *pot pourri*, and they can be used to ward off insects.

DILL
Anethum graveolens (Umbelliferae)
Annual

Dill makes a striking plant of about 90 cm (3 ft) high, with finely cut, feathery leaves. The flat heads of yellow flowers are followed by brown, ridged, aromatic seeds.

Sow dill in moist soil in spring, where the plants are to grow: they prefer a sunny position. A second sowing in early summer will provide a further supply of foliage while the first sowing is allowed to set seed. Do not allow the soil to dry out.

Uses: The delicate anise flavour of the leaves goes well with fish and vegetables. Add dill leaves to a dish shortly before serving as prolonged cooking destroys the flavour. The seeds are more strongly aromatic, warm and spicy; they can be added to pickles, bread and cakes as well as being used in fish dishes. Dill water is made by infusing the crushed seed and is often given to babies to soothe them and aid digestion.

FENNEL
Foeniculum vulgare (Umbelliferae)
Perennial

A plant which looks similar to dill, fennel is taller—up to 2 m (6 ft) — with even more feathery, thread-like foliage. The yellow flowers are borne in broad umbels from midsummer and set curved, aromatic seeds. Bronze fennel is a variety with dark, purple-bronze foliage, good for decorative borders; Florence fennel has swollen leaf bases which, in fennel's native Mediterranean countries, form a large, crisp 'bulb'. (In northern climates it takes a very warm summer to produce anything resembling this bulb!)

Sow fennel in spring in an open, sunny position in moisture-retentive soil.

Uses: Both foliage and seeds are used, the seeds having the stronger aroma. Their anise flavour is similar to that of dill, and fennel should be used in much the same way. The seeds aid digestion, and fennel is traditionally thought to cure a wide number of assorted ailments as well as protecting against witchcraft.

GARLIC
Allium sativum (Liliaceae)
Perennial

One of the most famous herbs, this member of the onion family forms a compound bulb containing several 'cloves', each of which produce tall, slender leaves growing between 30 and 45 cm (12–18 in). Small round heads of pinkish flowers may appear in a warm midsummer.

Garlic does best in the warmth of Mediterranean summers but grows reasonably well in northern climates. Buy a bulb from the greengrocer or supermarket and break it into separate cloves: plant these in well-drained soil in a warm, sunny position in late summer to overwinter. In heavier soils, plant in early spring. Harvest when the leaves begin to die down in summer.

Uses: The leaves are strongly aromatic and may be used in cooking to give a less pungent flavour than the bulb. It is the bulb that is mainly used, however, in almost any savoury dish. Use it very sparingly, for the flavour is penetrating and lingering. Garlic has been credited with dozens of health-giving attributes and is thought to be a good general tonic and guard against infection when eaten regularly.

The papery pink flowers of chives *(Allium schoenoprasum)* are particularly attractive and are very freely produced.

GERANIUM
Pelargonium species *(Geraniaceae)*
Perennials

The name geranium is, strictly, inaccurate, for these are the tender pelargoniums which need to be over-wintered in a house or greenhouse in cold climates. There are many different species and varieties with strongly scented foliage. They must be overwintered in a frost-free place and started into growth in spring: the best plants are produced from cuttings taken from the new young shoots. In summer they can go outside in pots or tubs. Flowers are small, white or pink and usually fairly insignificant.

Uses: The scents include lemon, balsam, southern-wood, peppermint, rose, apple, eucalyptus and clove: some are amazingly powerful. On most varieties, the foliage needs to be lightly rubbed before the fragrance is released. Apart from their uses in *pot pourri* and scented sachets, leaves can be used to flavour cakes and drinks.

HORSERADISH
Armoracia rusticana (Cruciferae)
Perennial

The leaves of horseradish look rather like dock leaves; they are large and coarse. Sometimes in midsummer white or pale pink flowers are produced in loose panicles: they are the typical four-petalled cruciferous flowers.

The roots of horseradish are large and very invasive; this is a plant that becomes a determined weed if it is not kept under control. Plant the roots in old bottomless buckets sunk in the soil, or in trenches lined with slate (traditionally) or heavy duty polythene. Rich, moisture-retentive soil produces the best roots.

Uses: Young leaves are sharp, hot and spicy, but they are rarely used. It is the thick, white root, peeled and grated, that gives us one of our most powerful seasonings. A traditional accompaniment to roast beef and smoked mackerel, horseradish can also be used to zip up many other meats, fish and salads. It is related to mustard and has the same hot, biting tang: it is far worse than onions for making the eyes water! Mix the grated root with a little vinegar and thick cream to make horseradish sauce.

HYSSOP
Hyssopus officinalis (Labiatae)
Perennial

A bushy plant with small, narrow leaves and blue, pink or white hooded flowers, hyssop grows to around 90 cm (3 ft) high. It likes a warm, sunny position in free-draining soil.

Seed can be sown in spring, or tip cuttings of young shoots can be taken in early summer. Established bushes may be clipped back in spring to prevent them from becoming leggy and untidy. Hyssop stands clipping well and can be grown as a low hedge.

Uses: Leaves are strongly aromatic, slightly bitter and somewhat minty. The flavour is strong, so hyssop should be used sparingly. It is good in sausages or with any form of pork, and is a useful herb for stuffings, particularly to accompany rich meats.

Tea made from the foliage is useful for coughs, colds and asthma; it is also a digestive. The foliage can be dried for use in winter (though the plant is semi-evergreen in reasonably warm situations).

JUNIPER
Juniperus communis (Cupressaceae)
Perennial

A shrubby conifer with whorls of spiky leaves: they are blue-green above and shining silver beneath. The tree grows up to 2 m (6 ft) or so in sheltered positions but can be low and spreading on the windswept downland that is its natural habitat. Many decorative garden forms have been bred.

Juniper is an accommodating plant and will grow in most situations, though it prefers sun and free draining soil.

Female plants bear berries which ripen very gradually, over two or three years. They turn from green to black, overlaid by a bluish bloom.

The feathery foliage and yellow flowerheads of fennel *(Foeniculum vulgare)* make this a valuable garden plant.

Uses: The berries have a strong, sharp, clean aroma: they are used commercially to flavour gin. Pick them when they are fully ripe and dry them before storing. Crush them lightly before use. They are particularly appropriate with game, but are also useful for winter soups and casseroles. Use them sparingly as the flavour can be overpowering.

LAVENDER
Lavandula species *(Labiatae)*
Perennial

The common lavender, *Lavandula angustifolia*, is a low-growing bush with narrow, pointed, silver leaves and spikes of purple-blue, highly scented flowers. It loves hot sun and is happiest in very free-draining soil.

Allowed to grow freely, it will reach about 90cm (3ft), but the stems will be gnarled and twisted, bare at the base and rather unlovely. To keep growth compact and bushy, trim the shrubs back fairly hard after flowering. *Lavandula spica, L. vera* and *L. officinalis* are synonymous with *L. angustifolia*. Good varieties include 'Hidcote', neat and compact, and 'Twickel Purple', with deep blue flowers. French lavender, *L. stoechas*, is a more compact grower: its flowers have large bracts and a quite distinctive appearance.
Uses: Lavender is *the* herb for scenting linen: it is also very widely used commercially as a fragrance for cosmetics. The flowers are at their most aromatic as the first buds on a spike begin to open; pick them on a sunny morning and hang them up in an airy room to dry. Use them in *pot pourri*, sachets and for scenting bath water (the name itself originates from the Latin *lavare*, meaning to wash).

LEMON VERBENA
Lippia citriodora (Verbenaceae)
Perennial
This graceful shrub, which used to go under the name of *Aloysia citriodora*, grows to around 2m (6ft) with long, tapering light green leaves. In late summer it bears clusters of pinkish flowers. It is rather tender, and though it may well grow outdoors in milder regions, there is always a risk of it being killed by prolonged or particularly sharp frost.

Take cuttings of healthy young shoots in early summer and overwinter these in a frost-free place as an insurance against winter losses. Grow the plant on light, very well drained soil and give winter protection: in cold areas keep it in a pot and move it under cover for the winter.
Uses: The leaves have a sharp, pleasant, citrus scent which will enliven a *pot pourri* or make an aromatic infusion. They can be added, finely chopped, to a variety of sweet or savoury dishes: as the flavour is quite strong, only small amounts need to be used.

LOVAGE
Levisticum officinale (Umbelliferae)
Perennial
This tall, stout herb is similar to angelica, with divided leaves and flowering stems up to 2m (6ft), carrying large, greenish yellow umbels of flowers. It will grow in sun or light shade, and likes a moist, rich soil.

The foliage dies down in winter, but strong young shoots grow again in mid spring. The foliage is sometimes attacked by leaf miner: affected leaflets should be picked off and destroyed. For maximum foliage, flower stems can be snapped off as soon as they appear, but the large plants can normally provide ample supplies in any case, and can be allowed to flower and seed.
Uses: Foliage and seeds have a strong celery or yeasty aroma and flavour and can be added to many savoury dishes. Use in small quantities as lovage can be overpowering: it is too strong for very delicately flavoured foods. Seeds are useful in winter when the topgrowth has died down.

MARIGOLD
Calendula officinalis (Compositae)
Annual
These very popular bedding plants are often called pot

Even a small garden has room for a herb border. Strategically placed stone slabs make all the plants accessible but are unobtrusive.

marigolds — not because they are grown in pots, but because they are used in cooking. There are many decorative varieties available. The leaves are quite large and coarse, pale green, and growing to about 30 cm (1 ft). Flowers, in shades of orange, are daisy-like with many petals. They are produced in great profusion above the leaves all summer.

Marigolds are very easily grown. Sow the seed where it is to flower in March or April and thin the seedlings as they develop. Make a further sowing in late August to provide plants which will overwinter and flower early the following year — though they generally sow themselves very freely in any case.

Uses: The petals add a golden colour and subtle flavour to savoury dishes. They can be sprinkled on salads or added to cooked dishes such as risotto, casseroles and soups, as well as puddings and cakes. Cooked petals look a bit bedraggled: you can infuse them in boiling water and strain the infusion into the dish instead of adding the petals direct if you prefer.

MARJORAM
Origanum species *(Labiatae)*
Perennial
There are several different marjorams, all of which have a warm, sweet flavour. The most commonly grown is sweet marjoram, *O. marjorana*, a tender perennial which is usually treated as an annual. It grows to about 25 cm (10 in) tall with small, mid-green, slightly hairy leaves and purple-pink flowers. *O. vulgare*, wild marjoram or oregano, is hardy and makes a spreading plant about 60 cm (2 ft) tall. It has a good, strong flavour; a golden leaved form is available. Pot marjoram *(O. onites)* is also hardy, slightly more compact, with a mild flavour.

Marjorams of all types grow well in a sunny position in light soil. Trim them back in midsummer if they become leggy.

Uses: Marjoram is particularly good with tomatoes, but is suitable for any savoury dish or salad, especially delicately flavoured meats. Sweet marjoram is a pleasant addition to scented sachets.

MINT
Mentha species *(Labiatae)*
Perennial
Surely one of the best known herbs, 'mint' may be one of many species, with widely differing foliage and fragrance. Nearly all the mints are very invasive, spreading by creeping underground stems. They are easy—almost too easy!—to grow, and need to be kept firmly under control.

Plant in moist soil in sun or light shade. Restrain the roots by planting within a bottomless bucket sunk up to its rim in the soil, or in a hole with the sides lined with heavy duty polythene, or use some similar trick to prevent mint taking over the entire garden. It has a disconcerting habit of racing along underground and popping up cheerfully several yards away where you don't notice it until it has thoroughly established itself.

The major disease is rust, which can be quite devastating. Look for rusty orange spots under the leaves; as soon as any are seen, cut off affected stems and burn them.

Good varieties include spearmint *(Mentha viridis)* with pointed, light green leaves; apple mint *(M. rotundifolia)* rounded, hairy leaves with a fruity scent; peppermint *(M. piperata)* deep, reddish green foliage, well-known aroma; ginger mint *(M. gentilis)* spicy mint scent and golden variegated leaves; and eau de Cologne mint *(M. citrata)* which smells just as you might expect. Pennyroyal *(M. pulegium)* and Corsican mint *(M. requienii)* are prostrate, small leaved species good for ground cover.

Uses: Mint is a good culinary herb, a traditional accompaniment to lamb. It has many other uses, though: try it in salads; with young, early summer vegetables (not just peas and new potatoes!); with any simply cooked meat. It can also be added to sweet dishes. Include the fruit-scented mints in *pot pourri* and sachets; hang it in the kitchen as a fly repellent, and use a bunch of eau de Cologne mint to scent bath water.

Armoracia rusticana variegata: variegated horseradish. The pungent roots of this herb are very invasive if they are not contained in some way.

MYRTLE
Myrtus communis (Myrtaceae)
Perennial

A sprig of myrtle was once traditionally included in every bride's bouquet. It is a rounded, evergreen, slightly tender shrub which will reach 3 m (10 ft) high in sheltered conditions. The dark green, glossy leaves are small and spiky: in summer creamy white flowers with bunches of prominent white stamens burst open. In warm years, bluish black berries follow.

Myrtle needs a sheltered place in warm gardens; in cold areas it makes a good conservatory plant. It can be propagated by semi-ripe or hardwood cuttings. Give plants outdoors some winter protection.
Uses: Foliage, flowers and stems of myrtle are all strongly and pleasantly aromatic. The leaves and flowers should be added to *pot pourri* and sachets.

Myrtle is not commonly used in cooking, but its spicy scent is appropriate to game and pork. The berries are also edible.

PARSLEY
Petroselinum crispum (Umbelliferae)
Biennial

Surely this is a herb that everyone knows! The frilly edged, tightly curled leaves are deep green and grow to about 25 cm (10 in): the compact plants make good edging. In the second year, tall flower stems with heads of white flowers are produced.

Parsley has an unwarranted reputation of being difficult to grow. Seed is slow to germinate in cold conditions, but given a little warmth seedlings can appear in days rather than the six to eight weeks usually expected. Make one sowing in spring and another in late summer: allow some plants to flower and seed and you should get a perennial supply of parsley from self-sown seedlings. If the early sowing is made in a warm greenhouse, it will germinate much more rapidly; it can then be planted out later (unless you are superstitious!).

There is a plain-leaved form of parsley sometimes known as Italian parsley, which has a good flavour and grows well in poor conditions.
Uses: Parsley is most familiar as an uneaten garnish—a terrible waste! Leaves and leaf stalks have a strong, appetising flavour and can be finely chopped and added to many savoury dishes. Parsley is thought to prevent the smell of garlic lingering on the breath.

ROSE
Rosa species (Rosaceae)
Perennial

It is the old fashioned roses that are most valuable as herbs, and there are many varieties to choose from. Most have only one, fairly short flowering season, but they make up for that with the quality of their blooms — usually large and blowsy, very strongly scented. Most are pink or white: some turn attractive shades of lavender, maroon and slate-grey as they age. Varieties of *Rosa gallica* are particularly useful. The hybrid sweetbriars, such as 'Lady of Penzance', have the bonus of aromatic foliage.

Roses like a well-drained, moderately fertile soil in an open, sunny position. The old fashioned type need only light pruning, removing dead or weak wood.
Uses: Rose petals are the basic ingredient of most *pot pourri*. They should be gathered just as the flower is fully expanded: if left until they start to fade, some of the fragrance will have gone. The foliage of sweetbriars can also be added to a *pot pourri*.

Rose petals can also be eaten. They have a light, delicate, scented flavour and are useful for decorating fruit desserts and cakes.

Rose hips are an excellent source of vitamin C and are often made into syrup.

ROSEMARY
Rosmarinus officinalis (Labiatae)
Perennial

Rosemary is an attractive, evergreen shrub with long, slender, mid-green leaves, silver on their undersides. In

Sage is one of the most decorative herbs, particularly in its variegated forms. This is golden variegated sage, *Salvia officinalis* 'Icterina'.

summer it carries pale blue, hooded flowers. It will grow to around 2 m (6 ft) in a sheltered position — it likes warmth.

Plant rosemary in free draining but moderately rich soil. Bushes can be clipped, and rosemary makes a good hedge in warm gardens. Propagate from semi-ripe cuttings in summer.

Uses: Rosemary is a traditional flavouring for pork and lamb, but can be used with any meat. The dried foliage is sharp and spiky so should be crumbled before use.

The aromatic leaves can be included in *pot pourri*, and an infusion makes an excellent hair rinse, leaving the hair lightly scented and shining. Rosemary can be used to scent many cosmetics.

RUE

Ruta graveolens (Rutaceae)
Perennial

'Jackman's Blue' is the variety you are most likely to come across—it is an intense silvery blue and makes an excellent 30 cm (1 ft) tall, decorative plant. The compound leaves are very attractive and in summer bright yellow flowers appear. Some gardeners think these detract from the steely blue foliage and remove them.

Rue likes a well drained soil and a reasonably sheltered position. It is usually evergreen, though a hard winter may knock it back. It is quite easy to propagate from soft or semi-ripe cuttings.

Uses: Rue is rarely used these days, and one sniff at the bruised foliage will tell you why. The aroma is intensely strong and most people think it unpleasant— our tastes have probably changed over the years! It has undertones of coconut, but is very distinctive; the taste is very bitter.

Rue has medicinal properties but can be toxic and must be used only under medical supervision. It can cause allergic reactions if handled by people with sensitive skin. These days it is grown as a decorative plant, though it does have insect-repellent properties.

SAGE

Salvia officinalis (Labiatae)
Perennial

The soft, grey-green foliage of sage, topped by spikes of purple flowers, make it an attractive evergreen shrub of about 30–60 cm (1–2 ft). There are several varieties with coloured foliage: 'Icterina' is variegated with gold; 'Purpurascens' is plum purple and 'Tricolor' is marked with cream and pink.

Free draining but reasonably fertile soil suits sage best. If it is cut back hard in spring it will make a compact bush, otherwise it is inclined to get leggy.

Increase sage from seed or from soft tip or semi-ripe cuttings. Coloured leaved varieties must be propagated vegetatively.

Uses: The strongly aromatic, slightly bitter leaves are excellent with fatty foods such as pork and duck (sage and onion stuffing is a traditional accompaniment). Leaves can be dried and crumbled to a fluffy powder which retains its flavour well.

Sage has been widely used as a medicinal herb, useful for its antiseptic properties. Sage tea help to relieve headaches and colds, and can be used as a hair rinse for dark hair.

SAVORY

Satureja species *(Labiatae)*
Annual and perennial

There are two types of savory, similar in appearance and flavour. Summer savory (*S. hortensis*) is annual and usually thought to have a finer, more subtle flavour than the perennial winter savory (*S. montana*). Both have thin, pointed, mid-green leaves on slender 30–60 cm (1–2 ft) stems with pinkish lilac, hooded flowers towards the tips. Summer savory is rather more delicate in appearance and is frost sensitive, while shrubby winter savory is largely evergreen in a sheltered position.

Both grow well in poor, stony soil, enjoying free draining conditions. Cut winter savory back in spring to keep it compact.

Sow summer savory where it is to grow in spring;

Salvia officinalis 'Tricolor', another variegated sage. This variety has green leaves marked with cream, or purplish leaves marked with pink. The small purple flowers are popular with bees.

winter savory can be sown in spring or summer, or increased by soft tip cuttings in early summer.

Uses: The savories are fine-flavoured herbs which deserve to be much more widely used. Traditionally, they are associated with beans of all types, but their warm, spicy, peppery flavour is also good with meat, fish, cheese, eggs and salads. The flowers are attractive to bees.

SORREL
Rumex acetosa (Polygonaceae)
Perennial

This relative of dock has arrow-shaped, fleshy, light green leaves growing in lush clumps. Flowering stems grow to about 1.5 m (5 ft) with panicles of reddish brown flowers that set into rusty seeds. The flowers are one of the least attractive among herbs, and flowering sharply reduces or stops leaf production: cut flower stems down as soon as they are seen.

Sorrel is one herb that likes light shade and a moist soil (which will retard flowering).

Sow seed in spring, indoors or where the plants are to grow. Plants are perennial, but are best replaced by new stock every few years.

Uses: This is an unusual herb in that it is not aromatic, but the young leaves have a sharp, salty, vinegary taste which is very refreshing. They make an excellent, clean-tasting early summer salad. Older leaves can be very lightly cooked (like spinach) to accompany rich foods. Blended with mayonnaise, they add a tang and an attractive green colour.

SOUTHERNWOOD
Artemisia abrotanum (Compositae)
Perennial

Southernwood is one of the most decorative herbs, with pale grey-green, thread-like, feathery leaves. It makes a rounded bush about 60–90 cm (2–3 ft) high. Very small yellow flowers sometimes appear in late summer.

Find southernwood a sheltered spot as it can be damaged by severe frosts. Soil should be freely drained but also moisture-retentive. If the plants get leggy, cut them back in spring once the leaf buds are bursting.

Semi-ripe cuttings, taken in summer, are the best method of propagation.

Uses: Apart from its value as an ornamental garden plant (the foliage is also useful for flower arrangements) southernwood is a good insect repellant. Include it in sachets for storing with linen. The very pleasant, warm scent makes it a useful addition to *pot pourri.*

The flavour is bitter and southernwood is not much used as a culinary herb, though very small amounts can be added to fatty dishes or strong-flavoured foods.

SWEET CICELY
Myrrhis odorata (Umbelliferae)
Perennial

Fresh, light green heads of ferny foliage and heads of frothy, tiny white flowers make sweet cicely a beautiful, delicate herb, usually around 75 m (2½ ft) tall. In soil that suits it, it can become quite invasive, making a large, spreading plant and sowing itself very freely.

Grow in a lightly shaded position and in moist soil. Although the plant dies down completely each autumn, fresh young foliage reappears in very early spring. Propagate from seed: established plants generally produce ample self-sown seedlings which can be lifted and transplanted.

Uses: All parts of the plant have a strong anise scent and flavour. The downy foliage can be added sparingly to salads, or cooked with sharp fruits like rhubarb, gooseberries and redcurrants to reduce their acidity and thus the need to add sugar. This makes sweet cicely a particularly useful herb for diabetics.

In winter the ripe seeds (which are carried in attractive, pointed seed cases when the flowers have faded) can be used instead of the foliage. Even the large taproot can be eaten, when cooked, in salads.

TANSY
Tanacetum vulgare (Compositae)
Perennial

The finely cut fern-like foliage makes tansy quite a

Tanacetum vulgare 'Crispen': this form of tansy has particularly good, bright green foliage.

decorative plant, but it is very invasive and must be planted where it can be kept under control. It grows to about 90 cm (3 ft) and has heads of round, button-like, bright yellow flowers.

Tansy will grow in most soils, and a fairly poor, dry position will help to check the spread of its tough, creeping rootstock. It is easily propagated by division, or from seed.

Uses: Tansy is rarely used as a culinary herb now because of its strong, bitter flavour, but it was once widely eaten at Easter in the form of pancakes or puddings. It was considered to be a tonic, cleansing herb which would purify the body after the winter: it does help to kill roundworms. Tansy has good insect repellent properties, and the strongly aromatic leaves can be hung in kitchens and larders to help repel flies, or included in sachets to store with clothes. The foliage also helps keep cats away from flower beds.

TARRAGON
Artemisia dracunculus (Compositae)
Perennial

This famous herb grows to a straggling plant about 75 cm (2½ ft) tall with deep green, narrow, pointed leaves and tiny, inconspicuous green flowers. There are two types of tarragon, the Russian and the French. French tarragon is generally held to have a much superior, more subtle flavour: Russian is stronger growing and coarser. Russian tarragon is easily raised from seed, while French tarragon rarely sets viable seed and must be propagated by soft tip cuttings or division of the rootstock. It is very difficult to distinguish between the two plants.

Tarragon needs a warm, sunny spot on well drained soil.

Uses: Tarragon has a pronounced, warm flavour and only small amounts are needed. It can accompany fish, meat and vegetable dishes and is used in soups and sauces as well as tarragon vinegar. It is particularly good with chicken. Russian tarragon, with its less spicy flavour, needs to be used in rather larger quantities than French tarragon.

THYME
Thymus species *(Labiatae)*
Perennial

Thyme is one of the most important and useful, as well as decorative, herbs. There are several different varieties, all fairly low and spreading, with small, tough leaves on wiry stems.

Thyme is a plant of hot, dry, stony hillsides, and it is in poor soil in a warm spot in the garden that the flavour is best. It is an excellent plant for growing in paving or on a wall.

Some thymes can be raised from seed sown in spring, while named forms must be propagated by semi-ripe cuttings in summer.

Garden thyme, *T. vulgaris*, has narrow, grey-green leaves and a pungent aroma, with pale pink or white flowers. Like all the thymes, these flowers are very attractive to bees. Garden thyme is easily raised from seed. The variety 'Silver Posie' is a small, slower growing form with mid-green leaves edged white.

Citrus overtones make lemon thyme (*T. citriodorus*) another good culinary herb with softer green leaves that make a compact mound. 'Silver Queen' is marked with silver, while 'Aureus' has golden foliage. *T. herba-barona* is an unusual, caraway-scented type forming a low, spreading mat.

Native wild thyme, *T. serpyllum*, is available in several varieties, including 'Annie Hall' with pale pink flowers; 'Albus' with white flowers; 'Coccineus' with crimson flowers and 'Lanuginosus' with woolly grey leaves and lilac flowers. *T. serpyllum* is another creeping, mat-forming thyme.

Thymes can be divided in spring or late summer; semi-ripe cuttings can be taken in late summer, and the low branches can be layered in summer.

The small leaves dry quickly and well, keeping their full flavour; they can also be frozen.

Uses: The warm, spicy flavour of thyme improves many dishes—all meats, vegetables, eggs and cheese. Flowers and foliage (especially of lemon thyme) are suitable for *pot pourri*. It is a strongly antiseptic herb—the essential oil, thymol, is still used medicinally as an antiseptic and a preservative.